When HUGO Meets Shakespeare

When Hugo Meets Shakespeare: Volume 2

ISBN: 979-8-9871406-5-9 (hardcover)
         979-8-9871406-2-8 (paperback)
         979-8-9871406-3-5 (ebook)

Printed in the United States of America

When *HUGO* Meets *Shakespeare*

Volume 2

Jean René Bazin PierrePierre

Table of Contents

Foreword

And the fiction goes on to please the so many
Who love to retrospect, whose peep is uncanny.
They love the true beauty set amid words and rhyme
And of course the travel back into the old time
That reveal the nature of humans as a whole,
The non-ending struggles that on them took its toll.

Though they are deja vu
Their style remains brand new.
And their shakespearean tone
Honors the names they own.

Carried so lovingly over the centuries
They flow and bring about the so many stories
Of a time of trouble, strong love and dilemmas
That mishandled, are still troubling the world karma.

Yet they still deliver.
Their rhymes strong and clever
Flowing, keen and witty,
Steal one's satiety.

So to one's enjoyment are set these lovely poems,
Reminders of that time that begot our problems.
They trickled down to us, heirs of candid errors
That set the world on fire for keenly they mirror
The ancestors struggles, fighting for sheer justice,
Amid a crowd beset with rampant cowardice.

My Godchild

You who so far ignore the magic of childhood,
Do not be so eager, my child, to come of age.
Of the many heartaches befalling adulthood,
Do not rush to savor the joys, sadness, and rage.

Your jolly years are sweet, worry-free but fleeting
Like a breath of fresh air, tomorrow is no more.
It fades, blown in the wind as time does its own thing;
It fades and, like the waves, eclipses on the shore.

Do not rush to begin to tackle grown-up tasks.
Do not rush from the pan, where you dream right out loud.
Do not rush up the time when you can freely bask
In your golden springtime, free of this life's dark clouds.

Time will make you mature and chase right from your eyes
The angelic aspect, the glare of candid soul.
Rather enjoy your world, tailor-made to your size.
Soon will come life tempests, soon, before you get old.

So go play, laugh, and run and draw from the fountain
Where the energy pours at every crack of dawn.
Go and enjoy your spring; other seasons will stain
From the blue of your sky to the shade of your lawn.

Oceano Nox

Oh! The many seamen and the many captains
Who took off elated, their dream goals to attain,
In the bleak horizon, slowly faded away!
How many disappeared, painful and dreary fate!
In a bottomless sea, on a dark, moonless date
Amid tarry waters, in ever-tumble, lay.

So many commanders dead along with their crew!
The tempest of their life destroyed their mere sinew
And, in a brisk sudden, made their faces paler!
No one will ever know how they drowned in the sea.
Every wave came engulf its part with no mercy.
One took over the skiff; the other the sailor!

No one knows of your fate, you poor forgotten souls!
You're tumbling all over the sea with no control,
Banging here, banging there, reefs and pitfalls alike.
Oh! So many parents cajoling the same dream,
Passed away while waiting patiently near the streams
Those to never come down the pike.

They speak of you often in any late vigil.
Many joyous circles on rusty anchors still
Bring back often your names, crown of a somber clout,
To laughter and refrains, to tales of adventure,
To the kisses your wives, lonely, have to endure,
While you rest lazily between seaweed and trout!

And they ask, "Where are they? Do they rule some island?
Have they forsaken us for some more fertile land?"
Then your mere memory, at the horizon, fades.
The body's lost at sea, while souvenirs awash.
Time, soother of all pain, any trace comes abash
And feeds the somber mind with sweet thoughts, ready-made.

Soon out of all sight, your faces slowly dim.
One busy with his sail; the other, with his steam.
Alone during those nights when thunder swings and blasts,
Your widows, old and gray, all tired of waiting,
Speak again of your names, all pensive and stirring
Souvenirs of a distant past.

And when they finally take their own one-way trip,
No one recalls your names, not even in a slip
From the mouths of sailors in some greasy tavern.
Not even a mention in some short article
Written of the new lands, now part of world circle.
Not even in old tunes, one's ears vaguely discern.

Where are they, the sailors submerged in somber seas?
O waves, you know so much of these wrecks we don't see!
Mighty waves, mere nightmare of mothers on their knees!
You tell them among you, riding away the tides,
And it's the sole reason your voices despair, hide
When you return at night to lounge by your chimneys.

My Children

All hopes, my child, remain like a willow.
God, in His hands, counts our days, my sweet dove.
He reels them off as tread so He can sow
On us kindness, mercy, patience, and love.
So to each below,
Death comes from above.

Yore, as you see, the future, blessed ray,
Often appeared to my bedazzled soul,
The starry skies and sea with waves that sway,
Radiant flower with beauty to behold,
But this bright display
Is now much too old.

If next to you laments a lone dreamer,
Just let it be. No need to find the cause.
Crying softens and often makes tamer
The one, alas! Upon whom fate repose'.
Teardrops make shimmer
What they so oppose.

My Dear

God who smiles and gently sows
And comes to whom for Him waits,
Provided kindness you show,
Will clean your slate.

The world where all things glimmer,
Where nothing's truly inflame',
If your loveliness shimmers,
With charm, you'll tame.

My heart, in loving shadows,
Bewitched by your lovely eyes,
Only if your smile aglow,
You'll mesmerize.

Written to Oneself

V

'Twas believed at that time, when the nocturne shepherd,
Far away, in the air, where not a sound is heard,
Would see, at times witness, by shadows overcast,
In a somber whirlwind of thunder and of rain,
Rapidly pass the face, as one with provoked brain,
Of a prophet carried by some spiritual blast!

There was faith in the days of the bard and minstrel!
When armed crowd would rise up and Calvary barrel
To free the holy cross
And see the somber lake where the Lord saved Peter,
The Horeb and Kidron and doors that time deter
To protect kings from moss!

There was faith at that time, when all led to prayer,
When Louis, at the time to take over Vallière,
Would stop deeply distraught before a crucifix,
When the altar would shine next to the gleaming throne,
When the king would utter, "Father, God reigns alone?"
The bishop would reply, "My son, He's the Matrix!"

The shepherds nowadays sleep down in the gullies,
Jerusalem's Turkish, harvests grow rapidly,
But reapers are no more.
The kingdom is falling; frustration is growing.
Alas! Now human beings dream while their faith's drowning.
Lord, who's better, therefore?

Quia Pulvis Es

Here they depart; there they remain.
Under the nor'easter's voices wailing demands,
Human beings, just as dust, all get carried away.
Alas! The same wind blows in the shades where we are,
Blowing on us though near or far,
Blowing on all things on its way.

These who remain to those who leave
Say, "O you wretched bunch! You whom your minds deceive.
What! You no longer will hear a word or a sound!
What! You no longer will see the trees or the sky!
Under the marble you will lie!
Under the darkness of the ground.

Those who leave to these who remain
Say, "Naught you have is yours! Your tears are averment!
To you, joy and glory are words of deception.
God gave to the dead ones the true lasting kingdom.
You, livings, are but real phantoms.
We, dead ones, are in elation!

To Viscount Eugene Hugo

Since the Lord saw it fit to crush you, O poet,
Since the Lord saw it fit, pain on you, to beset,
By the might of His will,
Within you build an urn, fill it with ecstasy,
Along with His Spirit and from His fantasy,
Give it His divine seal,

Since the Lord God bestowed on you deep mystery!
An undrinkable well, a voice with no query,
His breath on your forehead,
And like a drifting skiff, by waves overflowing,
Dragged your dear sanity despite you not knowing
Of the sea, the true stead,

Since He wanted your fall and, of death, the cold grip,
To make you live anew, setting you on a trip
Toward new horizon,
And since God set you up in this cage made of flesh,
Poor eagle, yet gave you wings for you not to mesh
Your soul with the reason,

You flew away, brother, adorned with your white robe!
You went back to your God like the dear spinning globe,
Remains upon its course!
You flew back to your Lord, with your candor as load,
Just like the treasured light and the air you upload,
All spring from divine source!

You had said nothing wrong, had done nothing of odd.
Just as a virgin dies, just as angels once trod,
So, young man, you took off!
Nothing sullied your hand or your heart in this vale
Where everyone hurries, forges, cries, and exhales,
You barely had a scoff.

And just like the diamond amid the burning flames
Disappear as a whole, with no trace to its fame,
Every eye to dazzle,
Just like a ray of sun when ends a summer day,
On earth, after you left, you left naught on your way,
Leaving us all frazzled.

Meek and blond companion throughout my childhood,
Oh! Tell me now, brother, laden with weight of wood
And a dreary future,
Tell me now, that since death has rekindled your flame,
Now that your soul aglow reveals nothing to blame,
You must have recaptured!

Tell me, do you recall the good old younger years!
When we were still drifting down the same current, dear,
Holding each other's hand,
When the great Napoleon would shine like a bright flare,
When we were all dazzled by his lusty fanfare,
Of his victorious band.

You must recall again the greenish Feuillantines
And the long corridor, witness of all the scenes,
Of our escapades,
Where in all the corners, the walls, and the fountains,
In the many bird's nests that the great oaks sustain',
Echoes that time can't fade.

O time! O lovely days! Memory so precious!
Why did God choose to give the life the most joyous
Early in the journey?
We were young, and it seemed the old monastery,
Seeing us so radiant, unveiled its mystery,
Of kindness uncanny.

Remember, my brother, right after we study.
Oh! How we'd be running in the fields, all shady,
By trees of any sort.
We'd run, chasing insects everywhere, jumping high,
With the grass, green and tall, way up to our thighs;
Then our thighs were still short.

Being two lively kids by racing all flurried,
Chasing down anything, in the air, so varied,
All tired at the end,
We would return, playing with all that we could find,
Elated and always, mother, alas, so kind
To kiss us both, would bend.

She would yell "Did you see what they did, these young men?
Monsters! They'll have picked off all apples. None remains,
But hey, we love them still.
Madame, men are always the worries of mothers,
For they run up and down and they just don't bother
Until they have their fill."

Then we'd sleep together, rocked by the dear hostess,
Who, in the same old bed, would soothe our early stress
Then rise at the same time.
We'd bite of the same bread dipped in the same warm milk,
The good and fresh-made bread on tablecloth of silk,
With appetite that'd rhyme!

And we'd gladly resume playing and making sheaves
Of the many flowers, from the green grass, retrieve',
Cuter than the other.
Mostly these bright flowers, so golden and lovely,
Shining all over town, sparkles of flame likely,
From the sun, left over.

And always together, joy of the family,
Of laughter flourishing, we'd run, bright and lively,
All under the arbor.
Alas! Alas! What grief to live on without you!
Rest in peace for now on, recover your sinew.
Here, I'll miss your ardor.

You'll be resting in peace upon this greenish mount.
And when winter whitens, with winds at every count,
When just the sky hovers,
All dust, you'll be resting upon your bed of clay,
And down there I'll remain, treading in my own way,
With what you left over!

There I will carry on, suffer, act, and exist,
While my name will climb up the long treacherous list
Of the celebrity.
I'll hide, like in Sparta, laughing up when exposed,
Every envious prong I carry well enclosed
Under humility!

I'll go back to my work, pick up right where I left,
Sail against the current, all weakened and bereft
Of what I so treasure,
Unlike the so many who sleep with no worry,
Just like a nest hidden far from the wind fury,
And death strongly censures!

I have austere hobbies. Just like a priest at church,
I dream of charming art, which ennobles and such,
Humanizing the world,
That, just like the sower, scattering the good seed,
While sowing sheer nature in souls striving with greed
Will make God's seed unfurl.

When at the theater are read my creations,
I come and sneak right in to hear the audition,
The big crowd, observing,
Over my tense drama whose foliage caves right in.
I hear run down their tears, just like downpour drops in,
The whole forest, drowning!

But what a dreading toil! All these waves! So much foam!
Mostly when pure envy, bitterness as its dome,
With sad and empty stare,
Turns, for the vile purpose of its vulgar attacks,
The lips of a dear friend, who last month had your back,
Into menacing flares.

What a life! What a time of turmoil! Where glory,
Power, genius, and faith, all that make history,
All that we hold so dear,
The little that remains of the waning splendor
Is trampled in the mud, pursued in corridors,
By snorts muffled and sere!

The river of slander! The torrent of vileness!
The many base pamphlets daily causing distress
To the one God begets,
Bringing him pure anguish, piercing with bought-up spear,
Just like feeding with gall the truth they so much fear,
Crucifying him yet.

How great is the fury set over the victims!
The so many rhetors dealing with precious themes,
Laughing with cruelty!
Seeing the strong venom sipping straight from their lips,
Drop by drop or by waves, when on the crowd they slip
Their vile impiety.

Humans seeking pleasure from every known corner
Mind the dolce vita and the place of honor.
Their new god is money,
Alas! Our passions, with their infamous snares
Where hang, miserably, the soul's forgotten glares
Of sacred harmony!

What's the use? Tell me now. What's the use for this hate?
Why spread so much evil and swim against our fate
When death in all parts looms
And will take anyone where everyone tumbles,
Where we fade in shadows and rest under rubbles
Upon which the grass blooms!

Why waste our energy in much sexuality?
Why waste our energy gathering wealth plenty
At the neighbor's expense?
Everything comes to pass. Naught surpasses its time.
When comes the great reaper, fortune's not worth a dime
In scale of final stance!

Whatever we pretend and whatever we are,
Beauty, richness, honor, what we uphold so far
And we pursue fiercely
Are scattered all over the fields and the meadows,
Blown away by the winds and thrown in the shadows
The world forgets swiftly!

And what a tiresome and mournful sensation
To see the piled-up crowd come up to your mansion
In these troublesome games!
Unchartered sea of minds with somber rolling waves
That comes circling around whatever the world raves
With sole aim to defame!

What clash of ambition struggling on the journey!
Everyone facing one, one facing so many!
What a tumultuous brawl!
How much scoffing is thrown at a declining star!
While nothing comes bother your dear forehead, thus far,
Wrapped up in your dark shawl.

There, in most treasured peace, rest in somber silence.
Every day, every night, in blessed remembrance,
Where the sun's lovely glow
Caresses from afar, with touch of gleaming hope,
Shining every aspect of your tomb on the slope,
The cross bright and hollow.

There, you no longer hear but the grass and the brush,
The steps in the soft ground, the gravedigger comes brush,
The ripen fruit's demise,
And every now and then, the tune, spread in the air,
Of the herdsman passing in the fields green and fair,
Herding his bovine prize.

The World and the Century

What are You doing, Lord, with Your dear creation?
What's with the river flow and the sea in motion?
The fields, the gentle streams quenching the sprouting grass?
And on every green shore, where all the herds come pass
In large crowd, all grazing and giving in return
To the soil the produce that they carefully churn
Chased around by the bark of overzealous dogs?
Why this autumnal land still cajoled by the fog?

Why this tender august, month of balmy weather,
With flowers offering, by breeze of the ether,
A warm and tasty treat to ever busy bees,
Changing every flower in cloche sweet and bubbly?
Why is there a fine mist rising from the hamlets?
Why the peaceful shadows lying under branchlets?
Why the placid blue lac, with isles all around strewn?
Why the thick of forest, the retreats, the caves hewn?

Why does the eventide in the late summer days,
Like a crimson backdrop when the sun fades away,
In the midst of the haze, dangling lazily still,
Seems to light up its last, gliding behind the hills?
Why ripen the old vine and shine upon the walls,
The golden rays cooking every grape in the stall?
Why tilt this blessed globe, on its axis hurling
And yet cradling softly all those cities, spinning?

This globe and its mountains and all its rolling seas,
Why then, O blessed Lord, rotate it so it sees,
Bathing in the shadows or baking in the glare,
The night with somber coat or the sun's gentle stare?

What good are for the gush, the cloud and clatter,
Which in fertile secret make the fruit that flatters?
Why then render fertile the heavens and the waves,
Clan in a world of suns that in the sky You pave,
Scattering with bright stars the dome of the heavens,
O Lord, and then beset on us the visual sense,
Enabling us to scope millions of joyful sights,
Sizing the horizon, sadly, our reach, alight?

Why when reaching the heights and in the depths as well,
One can see treasured sights or what shadows dispel?
What's the use, O my Lord, to nourish and nurture,
To love, cradle, and cense then always recapture,
For the deep perception as well as for the eyes,
What heavens patiently harbors for us as prize?

If it's for this era where the law is trampled,
Human beings go their ways shunning the Example,
Ignoring the message, belittling the warnings,
Refusing to follow the map of their blessings,
Given either by signs or uttered blessed truths
To lighten up their cross and all their sorrow soothe!

If this time will convert, in all of a sudden,
Yesterday's destitute to the rich so disdain',

That we clash ruthlessly over our many dreams
And the people trample the many sacred themes,
As well as the royals, staunch and severe lesson!
Make usage of brute force as their rooted reason
And reply as a herd, repelled with stones and killed
With weapons of fire, running or standing still!

If the stumping riot should shake the whole city
So that all be a threat, even sweet liberty!
If it's for the honor of the old gentlemen
Who themselves drove us there, refusing all demands,
To the party projects, remains sadly mingled,
If it's to one's hatred, an uttered oath dangles,
As though to add a blade to some ancient dagger,
If it is for the prince, that woman engender',
Born to shine up so bright but to live so little,
To believe he is king kept under Your mantle!

If it is that their joy, to the just ones eludes
So that iniquity reigns and envy includes,
Setting up many minds with fiery projects,
Demeaning many hearts that love would redirect!
If it is that the priest, sad, infirm apostle,
Walks around his domain, half blind as he bustles,

Real insult to nature, of the Word all conceived,
Unable to grasp that all, by the Spirit, live;
That God breathes life in us, giving life to the clay;
That the tree and flowers, the Gospel comes display!

If it is that no one, either old, either young,
Not even the elder, feeling the years' deep prongs,
Already perceiving, of the tomb, the cold fumes,
Has a calm disregard for the truth they inhume;
And like the ox plowing, lulled by inclination,
We furrow but ignore the real destination!

For the world, numb and cold and lacking reminders,
Loses the majesty of all You engender;
Humans no longer sense shine deep the heart candle,
The dawn or the lily, the child or the angel.
Neither soul reflection made of love's purest light
Or of the vast creation attesting God's true might!

All these often bring me to dream and think out loud,
"Will we be all condemned, lying there in our shroud?
Will all the human beings, with what they so gathered,
One day be forsaken from their dear forefathers?
O God, please have pity of people of this time,
Blindfolded, far from You, lost under their own slime.
Turn off the lights You send or rekindle their flame!
Take back Your creation or their soul, come and tame!"

In the Graveyard Of…

The crowd of the living laughs steady on its course,
Either for their pleasure, either for their sorrow,
But by the dead, silent, the ones we don't endorse,
As a dreamer, I sense their stare cold and hollow.

They know that I remain a solitary man,
Pondering all matters while strolling in the woods,
The mind that can capture, having so much to mend,
The trouble and the peace that every mind protrudes!

They know the attentive and careful attitude
I have when I'm around the crosses and the graves.
They hear me when I tread their silent neighborhood;
They see me contemplate where all the shadows pave.

They understand my voice, the whole world, poured over,
Better than you, livings, noisy and quarrelsome!
The precious hymns of love that in my soul hover
Are to you pleasurable, while to them, troublesome.

Forgotten by the world, they're embraced by nature.
The garden of the dead where we'll all someday sleep,
The dawn sheds a glimmer straight from divine pasture.
The lily seems purer; the birds joyfully leap.

That's where I spend my time, gathering white roses,
Consoling all the graves forgotten much too long.
I go, then I return until the gate closes.
I resonate the grass. For the least sound, they long.

I dream there, just drifting in a sweet lethargy.
I see, with eyes open wide on my every thought,
My soul slowly regain magical energy,
Mysterious reflection of what the world long sought.

All lost in my daydream, I vaguely see old bones,
Branches not really clear, shapes and flickering shades.
In the shadows, seated over time-bleached old stones,
I capture glowing rays and all flower parades.

There, the ideal daydream that my mind occupies
Hovers, luminous veil, between the earth and us.
There, all my ingrate doubts send prayerful replies.
What I begin standing ends in stance much pious.

Just like the thirsty dove in any rock corner,
Searching for some water at the crack of the dawn,
My ever-withered mind, as that of a loner,
Seeks for love, hope, and faith in the fair graveyard lawn.

Over a Popular Figure

You good folks! See this head where nothing good entered,
Under the stunning brow, dignified, ill-tempered
Of a tartar instigator,
In the mind where one day will spring all uprising
And will surface visions, the world peace dismantling,
Somber and troubling thoughts fester.

In India, so often, a curious bystander
Over a high mountain will, with respect, ponder
Its top, white clouds proudly crowning,
Looking at it afar, will dream and then believe
In its rocks and its streams and its forests retrieve,
The face of some god, there throning.

The inside of the mount harbors the deity.
Then comes up the big day of the solemnity;
They open wide the stony walls.
The folks rush in, running and shouting all the same,
The idol sought out, fetus monstrous and lame,
From inside the mount comes befall.

Pensar, Dudar

I told you already, the most dreaded disease,
The black cloud that the wind cannot just sweep with ease,
The heaviest burden, the most severe of pains,
That furrows our brows, makes us pale, dulls our brain,
That makes us see Hades shining bright on our walls,
It's the anxiety that our daily lives, stalls;
It's the fatal distress and the deep-felt turmoil
Causing our hearts to wrench and our soul to recoil.
And fate, one clear morning, still holding its tight grip,
Setting us face-to-face on this miserable trip,
Throws at us suddenly, lording over us all,
This mother of questions: Soul, what's your beck and call?
That's the ever dreadful and dark hesitation
That grabs, facing the world and its many nations,
The poor mind scrambled up, dumbfounded by the stress,
Not daring to say no, unable to say yes.

It's the infirmity of this, the human race.
So what are we sure of? Who will win in this race?
What is the quixotic, and what is the real thing?
When will heavens come down and solace to us bring?
Why is it that our paths, all by lies encumbered,
Trip us in every way? Why spirits so somber
Come frighten us at night, when it's time that slowly
The fog rises in hearts as in the sky, softly?
That even the clear dawn overcasts deep problems
And the whole world ponders, failing to settle them,
Even in the children, finding hidden pitfalls,
Doubts around their cradles as if they were but palls?

See, this man is so just; he is good and is wise.
No inner gall carried, of his heart changed the size.
If any deep sorrow his poor mind comes endorse,
Amid all his regrets, he's still free of remorse.
All the foes around him, if they come to his mind,
Are from their own hatred, not from his heart so kind.
He's a wise of the time of Aurele or Adrien.
He is poor, and it's fine. Nothing now can come strain
All the muted rumors in this peak of old age,
Nothing but his gray hair and his actions of sage.
Every human being for him sprouts of one Source,
And brother to the poor, he's the children's recourse.

He lives a simple life far away from the town.
In fields where all repairs, where all blots every frown,
The dancing villagers at the tambourine sound
A few ancient Greek books within whose lines resound
Athens or Laconia, all the heroes of old,
The children that you meet, with no reason to scold,
The dog you redirect and whose eyes understand,
The study of a bug busy in its errands
And at the falling dusk, bring home some friend elder.
This is, in a nutshell, of his day the slider.
Everyday, for daily, this is the way it goes,
When the sun retires, as well, he shed his clothes.
He joins back, evading the crowd wishing him well,
His terrace that winter covers with all tree shells.
And his table content, most of the times meager,
Brings to him the same smile, all jovial and eager,
The old and feeble maid who shuffles and staggers,
Whose strength and zeal differ but seem to still drag her,

Then he steps in the room with eyelids all laden.
And there, what does he do? In the old rustic den?
He with no desires, no faults, and no sorrow,
He thinks, he dreams, and doubts… awaiting tomorrow!

Somber fate! All's blurry and around all wavers!
Mostly that nowadays, when all's losing savor,
Where troubles come and grab the slowly drifting soul
And want to wreak havoc on what so dear we hold,
But the envious fate holds us back and nothing
But the unknown caprice that this life is swinging,
That a book old and torn, in some shadowy night,
That a thought cascading in an abyss of fright,
That a heart all ridded of the least illusion,
Weak vessel with no masts, over which the passions,
Seamen of misfortune, all troubled in their sway,
Stamping up, stamping down, trying to find a way.
When the only focus, in the last-ditch effort,
Looking for an issue, a direction, a port,
An anchor that secures, a beacon that directs,
What a dreadful feeling, with strong winds that deflect,
We bluntly realize that we walk without faith,
Yes, faith, this leading torch that settles all debates,
This word of hope written on the ultimate page,
This rowboat well designed to save the equipage.

How is it that we are, us so poor and foolish,
And again yet so proud? Say, you who try to reach,
You all branded by fate, soul always so serene,
To glory so modest yet to hatred so clean,

You with thoughts so even and of a mind so pure,
In the calm reasoning, this clear leading azure,
High and so far from us, shines bright and shines candid,
Just like a leading star in the blue sky, splendid,
Sun that is unbothered, for being out of touch,
By these troubled abyss, other planets, and such,
Where float, in every part, by some strong winds scattered,
Worlds of year of the light, with cultures all shattered!

Alas! How you must be pondering in silence
Over the so vain pride topping our ignorance!
How must you be laughing seeing our vain glory!
And just like the fire burns a smoke black tarry,

How our foolish pride, for heaven, sanity,
Must trigger in your soul a wave of strange pity!

Alas! Be merciful from your selected stand
For we hear everything but cannot understand!
This flagrant lack of faith, this wretched unbelief,
Ignorance or knowledge, wisdom or boast motive,
Is it, whatever name given to it by pride,
This century's failings or where every man slides?
Is it a passing prong or some eternal pain,
Where all is well written with the permanent pen?
God may have created human beings so heaven,
Hidden and mysterious, they study but in vain?
God beset us humans with nothing too certain.
To think is not believe. At times, through the curtain,

We hear a muttered voice not so clear but saying,
"Do not rely on it. Your work is not lasting!
Human beings build castles mostly standing on sand.
Back to oblivion, their work, nature resends,
And all the safe heavens where we bury our soul,
Glory, loud and flashy, love we just can't control,
The highest desires with glittering mantle
That just spreads all over flags of shiny spangle,
Richness ever fleeting and always alluring,
Science so hard to reach, with work so enduring,
Power with canopy, pleasure, under flowers;
They're all nothing but tents! The real building towers!
Stay away! Look instead for innumerable goods.
A tent, O you, mortals, helps only in the woods."
One hears this muttered voice and by it is branded
And perceives the heavens less far away, stranded.
Just like through a thick fog, you can discern the shores,
Almost there at your reach with promises galore.

But what? Yes, I often, with sight of an expert,
Dug in the dark issue, with mind of introvert!
These profound dilemmas with ever-changing themes,
Like the immeasurable sea, with clear or cloudy streams,
I searched high then searched low, but in neither I found
An answer to my plea, just worries much profound!

But I do certify, O winds of dusk and dawn,
To all the shining stars, my fondest oath I spawn,
With all the heavy thoughts trampling over my mind,
How often I have dared and attempted to find

Alone, fiercely searching some answer in the air,
Those heights where you perceive, of the world, the true glare!
The iceberg on the sea, the cape of desert sand,
How many times have I pondered in icy lands!
In the meanwhile, forests, rivers, fields, cities, ruins,
All left behind tucked in on mounts and in between,
Like gigantic censers, with smokes rising atop,
And the sea far away, rolling its dark flip-flop,
Shaping up proud reefs, standing so tall and sure,
Resounding strong and bold in its immense nature!

Then I spoke to the waves, "You waves, always rolling!"
And I asked the dungeons, with their towers falling,
"Towers, where is the past! Dungeons that every year
Comes nimble piece by piece with their teeth with no fear!"
And I said to the night, "Night full of shiny stars!"
I said to the torrents, the flowers, near or afar,
To all fruits and all shapes that death slowly decays,
To the mounts, the fields, and the forests, "Hey you, say?"
Many times at this hour, when the evening and wind
Push the lone traveler on his way, daydreaming,
That's when I asked myself, "This majestic nature,
This awesome creation set to serve the creature,
Knows all! All would make sense to whom who would fathom!
Just like the mute who knows the way to unbottom
A secret but remains, with lips torn and crusty,
Seems to attempt to shout, all eager and zesty.

But God forbids it all! In vain, you try to hear.
In those noises, no word from any other steers!

This tune that emerges from all the fertile fields,
Blended in the rumor that from the cities yields,
The thunders rolling loud, the winds with subtle wails,
The sea waves that recur and try reaching but fail
And go back and again return and start again
All these voices utter such an immense refrain!

Humans alone can speak and yet, alas, ignore!
Baffling limitation! Though dreamer in the core,
Everything remains sealed under a dour cloud.
And the soul leaving earth flies as though in a shroud!
So repudiate Rome so too reject Zion,
Laugh and lightly conclude with a loud negation,
It is so convenient, but so does the human.
Faith will always reflect the size of every man!

Since God wants it this way, therefore His will be done!
More of the true knowledge, solace, would have brought none.
Much often the branch breaks from many fruits laden.
What would become of us if the sacred hidden

By the sole Creator from His blessed Zion
Would have been, to humans, added to their reason?
The pot is too narrow to contain this great all.
It's fitted that each soul harbors a given small,

But dwelling in our sins, alas, to each person
Is embedded the choice: either faith or reason.
God! Death! Bottomless words well hidden in the mind!
The dreaded fright appalls every heart that it finds

Trying to surf abroad this deep dividing sea.
You don't cross it over. For any bird you see
Flying over these waves has to its wings, give rest.
Every lone traveler with the purest of zest

Trembles and hesitates at any given trip.
What soul remains immune to failures and hardship?
Children! Let us desist! Let's follow the journey.
The body bears shadow. The soul has doubts, many!

Tentanda Via Est

You don't have to worry, O sweet fretting mother,
Whose abiding kindness any trouble smothers,
Seeing him so little, so serious and pensive.
Like a frail little bird, alone on a reef, grieves,
Sees the swelling ocean, rising from down below,
He sees his life ahead with impending shadows.
He dreams of a future, treading ever slowly.
O sweet loving mother, don't you worry, really,
You, with soul whose nature's made of a charming blend.
The angel sees a child; the child, his dearest friend.

Come on, mother, freely, with a triumphant air,
Come give a sweet embrace to your most treasured heir.
He is not an expert, neither a prodigy.
He's a dreamer, better. Be proud and not edgy!
Contemplation, indeed, is a sign of genius.
Mother, the child who dreams is tomorrow's obvious
Thinker. And the thoughts swell and cover everything
And sent Dante to hell and Milton rejoicing.

One day, he'll be older. And a bright tomorrow
Is in store, you will see, for this child so thorough
Who wants to know the name for all he sees around
And so questions the world, every shape, every sound.
Who knows if he picks up from the ground, in solo,
The colossal scissors of Michelangelo,

He shouldn't, by leaving on the granite of wars,
Make a marble chiseled of dents worthy of stars?
Or like Bonaparte did or like Francis the First,
Take, as good chess players, Europe as board for test?

Who knows if he won't go, sailing at such full speed,
Adding up to the sight that his inner soul leads,

That telescopic eye, frightening the common,
Where the eye of the wise able to all summon,
Captures right from the sky or out of the deep sea
A star like Herschel or what Columbus did see.

Who knows? Just let him grow, this little serious man.
He seems not to notice our queries of humans.
Maybe this lonely child, already though fragile,
Has dreamed as often did once, as a child, Virgil,
At the trials undergone by the surging poet
That he, too, desires to tackle, win, and get
By some other pathway in this world we live in
That his name flits, hovers in every human scene.

April

Louis, the time is now for smelling the roses.
Let's open right out loud the blinds winter closes
And so admire, daydreaming,
All that Mother Nature displays as divine treats
That spring over mountains, all forests, and all pits,
Along water, shade, wind blowing.

Louis, the time is now for a soul makeover
In this subtle smile filled of flame undercover,
Shining deep in the sky so pure,
To open wide your heart like a steaming water
And let it rise way up like a cloud can scatter
And spread itself in the azure!

O Lord! Let the lovers under the leafy shades
Go around, all dampened by old winter tirades!
Let them wander, happy winners!
Let the nightingale sing, bird with a tender song
That brings out harmony, taking away all prongs,
Lifting the hearts of us sinners.

Let the wheat rise, let the child play, let water run,
Pink flower where sower dreams about catch that stuns,
Where all is laughter and prayer!
Where the greedy kid goat, all sneaky and agile,
Pulling low hanging leaves from tree with heavy pile,
Makes the goatherd watch for slayer.

Recalling past mourning, let's forget those we lost!
That under this blue sky we rejoice at all cost!
That young birds sing upon the trees!
And while all around us, all tremble and vibrate,
Let's go in the forest, as for a strolling date.
If you fancy, savor the breeze.

And we'll daydream about this beautiful maiden
Sleeping there on the grass, where buttercups glisten,
Where the bird feasts on the maple,
And who eager to have and who, oh sad story,
Had during last winter her mum's promissory
Word of a green dress in April.

Young Girl

Young girl, love, first of all, is a vivid mirror
Where a girl, flirtatious, delights in her picture,
And, full of cheers and dreams, comes peer.
Then, like blessed virtue, deep in the heart hidden,
Casts away infamy and vice back to their den,
Gives you a soul spotless and clear,

Then you go down one step, and you slip… And right there,
It's the abyss! In vain you try to grab the stair,
But you slide in, poor intruder!
Love is always charming, pure, fatal. Don't believe!
A young girl, by its stream attracted, is deceived;
She looks, gets in, then goes under.

The Strong Castle

What's wrong with all these waves, caressing tenderly
These coldly passive rocks, gleaming so brazenly?
What! Haven't they noticed, from foam on every face,
That these rocks, standing still and crashing their assault,
Have a fort as a crown, standing as a white vault,
Looking like a turban around their black tops, laced.

But hold on! Why should they harness their raging trend?
Come on! Throw your fury against this old foreland,
O sea! Give a reprieve to those weary seamen!
Nibble at this old rock! Make it stagger and lean
And topple finally, with its white fort so mean,
Headfirst in the waters and the fort and its men.

Say, how long does it take, O sea strong and steady,
To tumble down this rock and its fort already?
One day, one year, or more? Even a century?
Always crash at its base with your sandy waters!
But, O relentless sea, the time doesn't matter,
For a whole century can drown in your fury.

Swallow down this old reef! Erase it with your waves
And upon this pitfall, like rolling ones, behave!
Let all greenish algae come resurface its stand!
Let it lean on its flank, sleep in your somber bed!
That ever unnoticed, his fort loses with stead
A stone to every wave, tore down by your strong hand!

So that nothing remains, that the world feels slacken'
Not seeing the tower of Epirus's sultan.
That one day, on the shores trampled once by Ali,
If a seaman from Kos, sailing some starless night,
Notice a large vortex, stirring down, causing fright,
To the startled patrons, he narrates its tally.

Sweet Adèle

In the dark alcove
Near the meek altar,
The infant, like dove,
Dreams of shining stars.
While her eyes are closed
To this land, she chose
Heaven, so she rose
And away flew far.

There lost in a dream,
She gets to capture
The sand banking streams
Where shine all nature,
Suns with golden flames,
Strolling lovely dames
Cradling souls all tamed,
Basking in rapture.

She dreams in her sleep,
Sweet dream that enthralls
From the waters, deep.
She hears a soft call.
Siblings are around,
Father pacing ground,
Mother makes no sound.
She dazzles them all.

And she still marvels
At all that she sees;
Lilacs and laurels
Tickle her fancy.
Clear lakes of delight
With fishes in flight
And waves going right
Through willows flimsy.

My child, keep dreaming!
Keep sleeping, my love!
Your young soul's missing
Guidance from above.
But you drift gently,
Carried so softly
By the flow solely.
Angel that I love!

So free of burden,
You sleep all the way.
Nothing can pretend
To cause you dismay.
No pen, black or brown,
Has caused any frown.
Under your young crown,
Chase your bliss away.

Sleep, sweet innocence,
And angels, serene,
Who know in advance
Human future scenes,
Seeing you helpless,
Clueless, so stainless,
Willingly will bless
Your defenseless genes.

Since soft lips come brush
Her sweet, tender lips,
The child in meek blush
Calls him in her sleep.
But the strong angel
Then gently cradles
And, in a muffle,
Points to where faith leaps.

But her dear mother,
Hovering with care,
Comes quick to smother
Her passing nightmare.
And her proud treasure
That she reassures
Smiles back in pleasure,
Seeing her sweet stare.

Hidden Treasure

And when the child appears amid of his loved ones,
Loud cheers burst in the air, and his eyes shine at once
And make all the eyes glow.
The saddest of faces, maybe the most defiled,
Opened up suddenly at the sight of the child,
Happy, free of sorrow.

At any given time, like the green month of June
Or in bright November when nature is all pruned
With its days much cooler,
When the child emerges, joy usually follows.
With laughter and delight, we all observe the flow
Of his steps of toddler.

Often, we're discussing, facing a warm fire,
About God and country, where poets' souls fire
To the heavens, praying,
The child comes out and gone are heavens and country
And the holy poets! All blabber, running free,
Stops, with smile displaying.

At night, in deep slumber, when the soul takes its flight,
When you can hear whisper, as crushed under some plight,
The waves through the willows,
And if the dawn appears, true beacon, shining bright,
Causing in the meadows a fanfare by its light,
Where ring bells and swallows.

My child, you are the dawn and my soul, the prairie,
Whose essence of flowers embalms like a fairy
In everlasting spring.
My soul is a forest where somber branches sway,
Exposing playfully her soft murmurs your way,
With golden rays swinging.

For your frolics appease with unrivaled kindness,
And your hands yet supple, bearers of joyfulness,
Haven't caused any harm.
So far your little feet haven't stepped in mire,
Golden child of my heart, true flame of my fire,
Set with angelic charm.

You remain among us, of our arc, the sweet dove.
Your feet pure and tender, dusty grounds should not shove;
Fly around us instead.
With ingenuous stare, you question your domain.
Double virginity of body free of stain
And soul where angels tread.

It's such a lovely child with the most charming smile,
With sweetness of actions and voice where heavens file
Joys and shallow sorrow,
With sight ever roaming, delighted and surprised,
And spreading all around his young years as a prize
Next to kisses to blow.

O Lord! Save me from harm! Safeguard all my loved ones,
Brothers, parents, and friends, even the bitter ones
Around, hurting brethren.
Don't allow me to see a flower-free summer,
A birdcage free of birds, a hive free of murmur,
A house with no children

Quien No Ama, No Vive

No matter who you are, old or young, rich or poor,
If you've never calmly and patiently watched for,
One golden eventide, the sweet sound of a pace
Or a fleeting white veil, fading in the shadows,
That like a meteor with a bright passing glow,
In your quivering heart leaves a delightful trace,

If you don't even know, only to hear it said
By a poet in love, in some lovely tirade,
This blissful sensation that gives wings to the feet,
Of having a sweetheart, all faithful and caring,
Being your sole beacon, the only star shining,
In whose eyes rise and set all the suns love sees fit,

If you've never waited, all somber and dreary,
Outside a party, ringing loud and merry,
For the crowd to exit while you're drowning in stress
Just so you catch a glimpse, like a bright shooting star,
Of the crush of your life, the most treasured by far,
Walk by under the light, dolled up like a princess,

If you've never trembled of frenzy, deep and strong,
When the hand you search for, to other hands, belong,
To see your guiding light lights other pair of eyes,
If you've never witnessed, with saliva of bile,
A melodious slow, lascivious, and vile,
Where your cherished maiden is savoring her prize,

If you've never walked down from some lofty mountain
All exhilarated of some bliss just obtained,
If you've never tasted, under scented lime trees
At night when the heavens glitter its canopy,
Inspired, all enthralled, real life lovebirds' copy,
Well hidden, whispering, though alone and at ease,

If you've never felt weak holding that someone's hand,
If ever just one word that to each one we hand,
"I love you!" has not rung in your soul a whole day,
If you've never pitied all this world's great stories,
Thinking that while we seek fame, fortune, the glories
And the crowns; what a waste! When we have love at bay.

At night when the dim light twinkles down in the room,
When Paris lies, sleeping under nocturnal brume,
With the Saxon tower and the church of the goths,
Ignore, as the bells ring, the passing dark hours,
Which twelve times toll aloud, with uneven power,
Right out of the steeples, swearing unuttered oaths.

If ever you have not, at time when all's asleep,
When she, too, is sleeping, strolling in dreams so deep,
Sobbed like a weaned-up child from too much suffering,
Shouted many a times her name from dusk till dawn,
And believed she'd show up right there upon your lawn
And curse your dear mother and strongly wished dying,

If you have never felt that, from that one woman,
Staring deep in your soul, raise' another human,
That kept under her charm that the heavens open,
And that for this sweet child, playing with your feelings,
You'd have gladly given your life as though nothing…
You haven't loved as yet, neither suffered, my friend.

Beautiful Soul, Fitting Body

Madam, all around you so much grace shines aglow,
And you sing so lovely, and you dance just as though
You would melt the whole world.
A deep and moving stare gleams right from your sloe eyes;
Every inch of your being offers a soothing prize
Like the most precious pearl,

That when you come around, young star we admire,
Shine over all darkness with a smile that fires
Shock waves into our hearts,
Like the bird in the woods at the break of the dawn,
Tender thoughts emerging, spring from the heart fair lawn
Basking in rays you dart.

But you don't see all that; you ignore it, madam,
For your chaste modesty would chase any quidam,
Spreading its jealous veil.
And the chosen angel, safeguarding your sweet soul,
Never blushes of shame when, wistful, he takes hold
Of what your thoughts unveil.

Sinite Parvulos Venire Ad Me

Come on! All the children are good here. Who told you
That the breath I inhale, bringing me life anew,
With their naive breath, comes to crash?
Who told you their voices, their steps, their games, their screams,
Would, of my muse, trouble the slumbers and the dreams?
Oh! Come, children! Do come in batch!

Do come all around me. Come laugh and sing and run!
Your laughter will provoke some joy in me, in turn,
And your voices will charm my ears.
It's the source, in this world where all is causing frown,
That flows ever freely without bringing you down,
Nor to your inner soul bring fear.

Shame on you for chasing them! What is it you think
That hearing their laughter saves us not from the brink
Of some ever-impending gloom?
Do you think that I don't, at the sight of their games,
Rekindle deep within my inner drive all framed
By all these matters spreading doom?

Is your life so pleasant to your inner circle
That you choose to this crowd that joyously circles
And empty and silent quarter?
Do not come take away --for God, have some pity --
This blessed ray of sun, this shot of sanity,
The lovely sound of their chatter.

You'll drown mercilessly, in their loud frolicking,
The sacred words your muse, coming gently knocking,
To your soul chose to deliver.
But then I say who cares what she would come offer!
If I lose an instant as inspiring author,
I gain in heart jolly quiver.

The golden ambition and the rare destiny!
Singing loud and again wards of insanity
For lonely souls to put at ease.
To live solely on gall, bitterness, and trouble!
Pay daily for the dreams upon which you stumble!
Everyday tasting Charon's tease!

So much do I prefer my joy and my pleasure
And my whole family, essence of my leisure,
To the vain and fleeting glory?
Does my troubled poetry have, facing their laughter,
To quickly disappear, like school children after
A flock a bird in great hurry?

But no. When among them, I don't lose anything.
The gem of the orient flourishes all her strings
With golden flowers to display.
The ballad comes jolly with sparkles on its wings,
And the ode comes alive for lovely souls to sing
With stanzas flight in open sleigh.

They come freshly reborn from their flamboyant games,
And my sweet-scented hymns from the zest of their flame,
Perking up all the weary souls.
The bright and rich colors of childhood, my dear friends,
Instill in the verses a fresh dew kind of trend,
Just like the dawn in early stroll.

So come, my dear children! Run up gardens and stairs!
Shake up floors and ceilings, spill your joy in the air
From early dawn till the gray dusk.
Run around all you can like the bees in the fields!
My joy and happiness and my soul with no shield
Will follow lively when you busk.

To hearts truly deafened to all vulgar clamors,
Harmonious voices, chords, and subtle rumors
Captured only in the retreats.
Scores of great concerti often interrupted.
Winds, waves, and foliage that when the soul, prompted,
Turn subtly in musical treats.

Regardless of the world, the human, the future
That I have to forget or wholly recapture,
With or without my God's blessings,
I don't want to trample the world of the living
If not in a quarter where children are running
And freely their joy expressing.

And if ever I were to see you once again,
Sweet land of which language my voice sings in refrain,
Whose burbs my eyes have strongly stained,
Borders where, as a kid, I watched Napoleon,
Strong cities of the Cid, Valencia, Léon,
Castile, Aragon, dear Spain!

I don't want to go through your plains and your cities,
Cross over your bridges joining strong entities,
Roman or Moorish palaces,
And the Guadalquivir, winding itself away,
Only in the chariots, golden in their array,
Filled up with sleighing bell traces.

My Love Letters

O my dear love letters, of virtue and of youth,
Is that you! I'm drowning in your dear words that soothe,
All subdued, on my knees.
Bear that for just one day I come regain your size!
Let me please, so subtly, now much happy and wise,
All of my tears, release!

I was about eighteen, full of all kinds of dreams!
And my hopes lullabied me with lies in long streams,
Shining before my eyes!
I meant the world to you who I softly recall!
I was yet but a kid, but ashamed, most of all,
Now of my faded skies!

O sweet period of dreams, of strength and of graces.
Hope at every evening the sound as she paces!
Venerate a lost glove!
Demand it all of life, love, power, and glory!
Be chaste and be sublime and uphold the story
Of the immortal love!

But now that I have felt, have seen, have known, --So what
If I believe much less in the year of the cat
Than that of the rooster!
Oh! That this fiery age I thought was so gloomy
Next to the happiness I now feel flow through me
Give me now a booster!

What have I done to you, O you, my younger years,
That made you choose to flee, fly away from my sphere,
Thinking I was happy?
Alas! Now to return, beset with much appeal,
When you cannot ever give me back my lost deal,
Have I been that snappy?

Oh! When the good old days, the once upon a time,
When all was so lovely, so pure, and full of rhyme,
Come dock back to our shore,
We hang to every bit with warm and bitter tears.
And upon the ashes of what we once held dear,
We miss them even more.

Let us try to forget, for when the time has passed,
Let it carry as well the feelings of the past
To sweet memory land.
Nothing remains standing of what we once have been.
We become a shadow lost on this life big screen,
So just follow the trend.

In God Is All

To you who for so long, in my proximity,
Saw shine the blessed days bringing prosperity,
You who when my poor soul, wavering in its core,
Devoid of the least hope, asking the way encore,

While resting on your breast nursing my somber dreams
And at any instant would burst in jovial screams,
Alas! My dearest friend, alas! Now the shadows
Has invaded our world, and life's dull and hollow.

Now that dreary sadness has bent over to stroke
The screen of our azure and in us gloom provoke,
Now that our dim eyesight, losing what once perceived,
Searches a horizon so hard now to retrieve,

But in this somber sky, spreading its vale around,
Like a bright, shining eye, alive and well abound,
Can you see over there, deep in the sky, that star?
From the so many truths that heavens keeps afar,

That one is now revealed! It is the very first
That on us here below, its golden light has thrust!
Our sky well enrobed with its somber mantle
Failed to hide the bright glow of its golden sparkle,

And from the four corners of this huge firmament,
The darkness will come down but cause enlightenment.
And the darker it gets and the somber shadows
Come shroud the world around with gloom and with sorrow,

The more in the heavens we will gladly catch sight
Of the many blessings and splendors shining bright!
Then we'll see in the night, right where they all gather,
All the essence to hold, gleaming all together

And revolving around some compelling center,
Break and then reconnect their innermost twister!
In this terrible night of dreary misfortune,
We can catch much clearly, sight of humane fortune.

It displays at both ends, written in words of fire,
These words: "Immortal soul! Power ever higher!"
For as long as the day shines its sun bright aflame,
It overwhelms the eyes, and the soul, renders maim.

And we rest in a doubt, as troubling and poignant,
Not knowing if heavens is alive or dormant.
But the night opens door for shiny stars to glow,
Like flickering candles God lights for us below.

The eye captures within the vast dome all-somber
Thousand of bright new worlds it once failed to number,
Ever glimmering stars, so much brighter at night
That in the dark azure, shine bright to our weak sight.

Disdain

I

Who can precisely guess the many jealous thoughts,
Of hatred, of envy under all the hats brought,
Of muted resentments, of animosity,
Of storms to unsaddle the proudest of riders,
The profound emotions, the fury, the spiders
Crawling around your world of sensibilities!

But you ignore it all! While steady at your feet,
The mouths of deadly snakes get crushed in their defeat.
And all these cold rivals of whom you thought so much
Come and swarm all around and, in the dark of nights,
Dig all kind of pitfalls while you walk with your sight
Set upon matters unlike such.

Or if sometimes they howl for your soul to perceive
And your anger rises and, soaring high, you seethe,
So ready to smite down the horde calling your name,
Right before you erupt and scorch them to the core,
Right before your last growl, when all about to soar,
You smile and simmer down, soul all gentle and tamed.

Then you gladly return to your dear reverie,
Family, infancy, love, God, and sweet country,
Lyre to tune anew and stage to spring to life,
Napoleon, this god of whom you'll be singing,
The great men always scorned by those who saw them spring,
All, of wisdom always so rife.

II

Go ahead, deadly foes of his name! Foolish crowd!
All around his genius, your jealousy, avow!
Keep it going steady! No break and no remorse.
Don't you ever give up! Do it relentlessly,
Give it all that you got, do it over fiercely,
Envious! As poet, he dreams and sleeps, of course.

Your clamor that sharpens, vibrating like a sword,
Is but an added sound in all that from him soared.
Fame is a great concert of an echo widespread,
Horde of demons, blissful accords, angelic host
Sounding like a racket from lots of bikes' exhaust
At a gathering of skinheads.

He knows not about you. Once in a while, he says
That male cicadas thrill throughout all summer days.
That thorns to each flower, that it's just common fate,
That it'd be a pity, a cicada to crush,
That too much good is bad! That there's a thing as such:
A no-thorn rose will spring from no-perfume rose slate.

Then who cares! Friends or foes, all of them ends one day.
Deep within the same tomb is where we'll go someday.
Nothing troubles a soul all branded with God's seal.
Thrones, scepters and laurels, temples, and victory,
To regents in power, we'd give crowns of glory,
From what to him has no appeal.

So what can your howls do, hoarsening all your voice?
The waves come all crashing, not given any choice.
He doesn't know of you and really can care less.
In trying to bring down what he easily builds,
You're sweating big bullets, irritating your wheals.
He ignores the reasons you appear so hopeless.

III

Then when he'll be ready, writers, doctors, poets,
He knows well that he can, with a word of him yet,
Shut all your clamoring
And that he will carry all your voices away
Just like the sea's strong breeze dissipates on its way
All sailors caroling.

In vain, all your legions, circle close around him.
Just one effort he makes will unravel the schemes
You're plotting all around;
One single word from him, your feeble noise, covers,
Just like the thundering of chariots can hover
Bumblebees' buzzing sound.

When he wants, your torches, the sublime aureoles
That brighten your temples and adorn your idols,
Your gods, and your lobbies,
Ever dazzling beacons, universal clearness,
Fade next to the sparkle fizzling from the brightness
Of his smallest ponies.

To a Traveler

My friend, you just returned from one of these long trips
That make us age so fast and of foolishness strip
At a pretty young age.
You ran the seven seas in your feverish race.
Alas! Of your voyage the world could see the trace
From your boat the mileage.

The sun of many skies has matured your forehead.
The weight of fickleness so steadily has led
You down here and up there,
Just like a true plowman who sows after he reaps.
You took in those places, and you allowed to sip
Your soul, in trade so fair.

Whereas your friend settled, less fortunate as he,
For the so steady flow of life's dreary journey
In the same horizon,
And like the standing tree, the accent of its line,
As shadow for his porch, has its roots well define',
Sharing his same seasons.

And you returned weary from all those folks you met!
So you came back at last, tired but willing yet
To come rest in your God.
All sad, you're telling me your senseless endeavors,
And your feet mixed their dust, all tired retrievers,
With ashes of my pod.

But now your heart's laden with what really matters,
With the children around, you unfold your chatter,
Brushing up their blond hair.
And you're asking of me, painful solicitude,
"Where are your mom and dad? Your son, my eyes, eludes."
They've flown where no one dares!

They flew to foreign lands with no sun and no moon;
You only travel there after carefully prune
What the Master rejects.
The trip they undertook is deep and has no end.
You take it steps by steps, and no one can pretend;
No one dares interject.

I bade them sad farewell, just as I once did you.
And over the seasons, for the old like the new,
Gently they departed.
Alas! I buried deep at that fatal hour,
The so precious treasures, my heart to devour,
Miser so coldhearted.

I watched them all depart. Three times a somber shroud,
Wrapped each precious body. I was left with a stroud,
My weak self to console.
I wept holding their hands turning numb, turning cold.
Then I was left with none but this image to hold,
Their soul flights that cajole.

Yes, I saw them depart like three lovely swallows
In quest of better skies with much brighter rainbows
And steadier seasons.
My mother saw heaven and was first to ascend.
The bright glow in her eyes that she could not pretend
Gave no doubting reason.

Then it was my firstborn who followed, then Father,
Proud veteran laden, of every known feather,
With forty years of war.
Now they all rest in peace, in everlasting shades,
While their soaring spirits join the peaceful parade
While we tread not too far.

If you fancy later, in the night quiescence,
We will together go on the vale prominence
Where all my elders rest.
You will catch sight firsthand yourself, my dearest friend,
From the town and the grave that can better attend
To the loads on their chests.

Let's go, and in silence, ears tight against the ground,
Let's listen as Paris has muted all her sounds;
We'll listen carefully.
All the souls departed that the Lord has to glean
Come up from sepulchres, all confused from the scene,
Like grain to be tallied.

So many happily live their lives and forget
The ones that were once dear, hearts' favorite targets,
Trampled down over years.
The dead live a short life. Leave them in the cold tomb.
Alas! They'll stay buried in the earth's gentle womb
More than in our minds, dear.

So, friendly traveler! We can be so foolish!
Who can tell the many of the ones once cherish'
Drop from our memory?
Who can tell the reason the sorrow fades away
And why the so dense grass, over time, come what may,
Every grave, comes bury?

History

The fate of the nations, just like the deep-blue sea,
Has its hidden pitfalls and its moving chasms.
Blinded remains the one who always fails to see
In the lots of the world the many wave spasms.

A strong and immense flow moves throughout these great storms.
A ray of sun pierces the shadows of this night.
And when mixing death bawls to joy cries is the norm,
A subtle voice whispers within this troubling sight.

Centuries all alike, centenary siblings,
Different in their fortune but alike in their hope,
Find a similar aim through much different dealings,
And their various beacons shine from up the same slope.

II

Muse, there is no era that your sight cannot scope.
Of the merging future, you trail solemn circles.
For the days and the years or centuries won't cope
At leaving mark in stream that forever trickles.

You, hangmen, have no doubt, have no doubt, you victims!
She carries all around her ever-shining light,
Hovers above mountains, dives in deepest of streams,
And often builds temples where sepulchres alight.

To forgotten heroes, she brings the glorious palm.
Of conquerors' chariots, the frail axle, ruptures.
Of falling empires, she daydreams with no qualm,
And in all her roadways, God's teachings she ensures!

Of the old-time castle, she settles the summit,
And centuries convene at the sound of her voice.
Her hand, like a loser ashamed of his defeat,
Drags the old past up to the futuristic noise.

Collecting the wreckage, over the world scattered,
She follows all around the humongous vessel,
Knows well how to capture, from eras unchartered,
From the very first tomb to the last one nestled.

To My Odes

My odes, now is the time to spread out your wings.
Ascend all together to the heights of love springs.
Now it's the perfect time… Let's go!
The thunder brightly shows the way,
And the tempest of nowadays
Swings to the northern winds that flow.

For the one who longed for the day of sacrifice,
The time the storms set in always rolls the right dice.
But I, under favorable sky,
If ever, genius fortunate,
Had seen your blue robes fluctuate,
When the harmonious light went by,

If any profaner meddled in what you bring,
If any vile reptile had dared trouble your strings,
Crawling over their chaste luster,
If the world, as it saw your charm,
Had not come willfully disarm
From the ecstasy you foster,

I would have blest my muse and claimed sweet victory,
Would have told the poor poet, launching for sheer glory,
"O dear brook in search of the sea,
Flow to the ocean of the world.
Don't be afraid to come unfurl.
The waves are not too rough, you'll see."

II

Blessed is he who stands up to his lapse shadows!
Blessed, if he ignores all the mournful echoes
That a name can make resurface!
If glory comes with its concerns!
If in the dear poet, you discern
The chosen martyr of a race!

Not minding the hunter, the storm, the fear of heights,
Happy the bird that flies, flitting to its delight!
Happy who tempting will not dare!
Happy who follows as he's told!
Happy who lives and would not scold,
To sheer delight gives all his care!

III

O you, my odes, farewell! Of your own wings go rise!
Soon, knocking at my door, making resound your sighs,
You will mourn, missing terribly
The time when, hidden under veils,
To us you would come and unveil
Stars of heaven, glowing wobbly.

When, in turn, we would take the throne of the audience,
Of few friends gathering, weighing you in silence,
Poets moved with inspiration,
Running away from the town's brine
And who never failed to define
Their talents through their quotations.

Like angel hovering and spreading golden wings,
You'd come just to reveal sacred truths in wordings
To exhort and then to deceive.
You would say in your steady flow
All that can transform the morrow,
All the dreams the soul can conceive.

In healthy arenas, in some noble contest,
To sons of Hippocrene, when you'd allow the test,
Challenging your gentle essence,
Just like Atalante's lover,
Before their display was over,
You would distract them in their stance.

They would see you go by with sylphs and with fairies,
Wrapping your ancient beams to all our young trophies.
Sing the prowess of all their work
Or give loud cries of prediction
Or ask to the gothic nation
Their old tales, always full of perk.

Often your soothing lutes would come and ease their loads,
And from the heights of stand you'd protect their upload.
Often helping the innocent
As expiatory tribute,
You would mix, nimble and astute,
Tears to blood so it'd be decent.

IV

And now it's all over, and just like the swallow,
Please go! And go attend to similar sorrow.
And I, as long as in your fights,
Of your true motive no one doubts,
And that a soul silently shouts
What from you would set them alight,

As long as on the sea, churning from many streams,
The tempest will propel your sails devoid of steam,
That one true friend, feeling sorry,
Seeing you battling the strong winds,
Would set a beacon by all means
To drive you from the storm's fury.

I would feel much less sad knowing of your wrecking.
But now it's late; depart! No need to stay moping.
We have to tackle wickedness!
The lyre remains just a spook!
God, present just in every nook,
Sets up all odes with blessedness.

V

The poet so inspired when his world's unaware
Resembles mighty heights that the new dawn ensnares
And so gilds before he awakes
And that always dispels shadows
And safeguards through the dark hollow
The ray of sun he freely stakes.

The Genius

Circumstances don't make the man.
They only put him in display;
They just unveil, to put it plain
The genius's kingdom he once laid,
The resource of a past era.
Those nameless and forgotten kings
Who really rule by their aura
And the power of their thinking,
Chosen based on conjuncturas
In need of one to lead the course,
They spring from no predecessor
And beget no posterity.
Of their race, the sole professor,
Once they performed all their duty,
For the future, they leave recourse…F. de la Mennais.

I

Woe to the child upon this earth
Who in this unjust and vain world
Carries a soul inside his girth
Likening heaven's precious pearl!
Woe to that child! For vile envy
Would swoop down fiercely and heavy
Just like the eternal vulture
And of his success, so annoyed,
On this new Prometheus's joy
Will come shower all its censures.
Glory, this celestial phantom,

Appears far away in his sight,
Ready to infuse martyrdom
With smile imperious and bright!
So the swallow, meek and timid,
Tries to flee from the luring lead
From the hydra persistent charm.
It flits swiftly from peak to top
But still finally comes and drops
As victim, by sweet glance disarmed.

Or if at last the rise of dawn
Gilds the bright day of his efforts,
If yet alive, it comes and spawns
Laurels and prizes of all sorts,
Error, the haughty ignorance,
Unpunished insult, hate, outrance
Wear down the days of the genius.
Of misfortune, striking sample,
Glory leads him to her temple
As martyr for rites religious.

II

But then must one fall as victim
Of injustice or of sorrow
Who wouldn't gladly take the steam
Of glory at the price of woe?
Which mortal who feels deep inside
Shine bright a flame he cannot hide

That the time span cannot injure
Would, like dreading his victory
Amid this nonending glory,
Shun his sad and noble future?

Chateaubriand, I bear witness.
You, sent to mingle among us,
Bestowed with this gift of fondness,
Scorching egos too envious.
When your name spans across the years,
Why bother, despite all their spears,
You, giant, with hordes of midgets?
All to the genius owe tribute.
Their libel is not so astute
How venomous as they can get.

Face up the hatred infection!
The drown mocks the flowing waters
When its stern, in jubilation,
Enters the wharf, clear of blasters.
From the world, ignored for so long,
Your skiff is now where it belongs,
Far from the waves and their menace.
Homer, like you, back in his days,
Upon the earth would roam his way
Then one day lead the human race.

III

Still young yet, when from hands of crime
France, in mourning, received her loads,
You fled. But the spirit in time,
In you shone in other abodes.
Contemplating those vast seashores,
Those great rivers with woods galore,
To the world your farewell you said,
For in those sites unknown to man,
At least traces of God remain
Still untouched by man's petty raids.

You came at a much calmer time,
Tread that country, land of the arts,
Where grows Virgil's most treasured prime,
Where tumble all Caesar's ramparts.
You saw Greece all humble and tame.
Alas! Tyrtaeus can't be blamed
For these people so famous once
Now the Greeks bow meek and docile,
And the Thermopylae's turnstiles
Bear of their tyrant the strong bonds.

Those cities of strong history
Wail for their long-lost warriors,
And the remnants of their glory
Render their aspects sorrier.
The gods have fled, and their prairies
Farewell to the white theories!

73

No more games, no holy concerts!
Farewell to the fraternal feasts!
And the Dardanelles blowing beasts,
Their temples turn into deserts.

But if Greece lost all her prestige,
You knew of the majestic sites,
Where was the most sacred vestige
That through the years have kept their might.
A tomb yet full of energy
And Jerusalem on her knees,
By some pasha freely trampled,
The Bedouin, son of Numidia,
And Carthage and old Phoenicia;
All whose treasures kept great samples!

Back finally where you belong,
You returned, bringing as treasure
Your pain, results of foreign prongs
And great study of the future.
So your lyre you put to rest.
Then in your mind, reason came nest.
At the senate, rang in your voice.
Therefore freedom, all reassured,
Into your hands, her case ensured,
Now defender of kings by choice.

This arena where you excel,
Be proud to have well fought the fight,
Honored for having been compelled
To be genius and ideal light.

Pursued, fill all of us with hope.
Serve your prince and help France to cope
When she faces up destiny.
Anarchy, mighty and menial,
Trembles in its petty denial
Before your keen eye's scrutiny.

Let envy, with all its perverts,
Chase you down with its vile clamors.
Your noble flight, genial expert,
Smothers its miserable rumors,
Just like the albatross wandering,
Seeing the clouds, above running,
Defiant in their mighty float,
For it, away from earth rumble,
Gliding the air free of tumble,
Falls asleep without taking note.

Moses over the Nile

"Sisters, the water's cool at the first rays of dawn!
Come on! The sower still has not troubled the lawn.
Of life the shores are yet bereft.
Memphis barely murmurs some chatter too feeble,
And of our chaste pleasures, nothing will go trouble,
Except the dew the night has left.

"At my father's castle, glitters the works of art,
But these costal flowers much warmth to me impart
Than porphyry or golden pond.
These aerial hymns perceived are my favorite concert.
I prefer to the fumes of incense of experts
The zephyr's flow so vagabond.

"Come on! The water's calm, and the sky is so clear!
Leave under these bushels, hanging all our shawls here,
With all the ornamented belts,
Detach the tiara and the long silky veil.
Today, in the waters, let's remove any bale
That in the past we must have felt.

"Come on, come on! But look, amid the morning mist,
What is it? Scan keenly the horizontal piste.
Do not be afraid, my ladies!
It must be some old branch of tree from the forest
Gliding down the waters. Let's pay attention lest
We become part of its trophies.

"What to say? I don't know. I can't believe my eyes,
It is Hermes's bark or the conch in small size
Of Isis, pushed by a light breeze.
But no, it's just a skiff, or in a peaceful stance,
I can see a baby sleeping in sweet cadence
As though sleeping in mother's ease.

"He's sleeping. From afar, his floating crib, seeing,
You would think you had seen, on the waters, straying
The fragile nest of a white dove.
In his infantile bed he drifts, pushed by the winds.
The waves rock him. He sleeps, and the gulf, while stirring,
Seems to rock his tomb though with love!

"He's waking up! Oh come, you virgins of Memphis!
He cries... Ah! What mother could leave her son like this,
To the mercy of the waters?
He stretches his arms. And waters thunder around.
Alas! Toward his death, he was set to be bound,
With only shield a reed cluster.

"Let's save him... he may be one of Israel's sons.
My father censures them; oh, what wicked person
To so censure the virtuous!
Poor baby! His fortune has melted all my heart.
I want him as my son. I'll give him a good start
Though he's not from my uterus."

And so uttered Iphis, hope of the mighty king,
While on shores of the Nile, her escort quick to bring
All help to her swift decision,
And these lovely beauties following her with pride,
When this royal princess would unveil, like a bride,
Think they'd have a nymphal vision.

Under her precious toes, the whole river quivers.
All trembling of pity for the baby's whimpers,
Leading her in her timid walk,
She cradles the frail skiff, weighing its subtle load.
Her poise of yesterday, of fearful royal code,
Is tackled by virtuous balks.

And soon through the waters and the broken willows,
She now carries slowly the baby from the flows
To the wet sand on the seashore.
Her sisters in a file, on the newborn's forehead,
Hovering their sweet smile on his pulsating head,
Would shower soft kisses galore.

Now come, you, from afar, you in your cruel doubt,
Who followed up your child with hidden divine clout.
Come closer, like a true stranger.
Don't be scared! Come closer! Hold Moses in your arms.
The tears of your rapture will not reveal you charm
And put your poor life in danger.

While radiant of bliss, with a true winner prance,
The virgin to her king carried the future prince,
Meek and wet from maternal tears.
You could hear the chorus in the heavens above
Of angel hosts to God, in chants, sending their love.
Now the fierce king should start to fear.

"O Jacob, mope no more! For here in your exile,
No more your tears may fall in mires of the Nile.
The Jordan longs for your footsteps.
The great day soon will come when to that Promised Land,
Jessenia will witness, despite their foe's strong hands,
Escape the tribes with joyful pep.

"Under the frail aspect of a baby afloat
Is Sinai's chosen who, all severe plagues, denotes,
By virgin rescued from waters.
Mortals, laden with pride, who shun the Almighty,
Bend the knee for a crib from God's blessed pity.
All your shackles will soon shatter!"

Before a Rhône Glacier

Often, in my mind, rich of metamorphoses,
When I slumber on themes that the world encloses,
God, everlasting Light, that the world cannot see,
Mysterious Sunshine, inner Light of the soul,
Sheds a ray of His light and comes and takes control,
Wrapping me in His great mercy.

Right then, my poesy, as a cloud drifting high,
Whimsically dallies, wandering in the sky,
From all the four corners of this most precious globe,
And looking from up high, from these radiant vaults,
The cities of the world, and with scornful assaults,
Throw them her shadow as a robe.

Then at the golden dawn, bright in its morning glow,
She either cuts a piece of its veil spread below;
Or like a warrior stomping loud in his ranks,
She lightning-strikes bluntly the forest in slumber
Or restores her armor, of the red and somber,
Of the eventide daily pranks.

Then over an old mount, giant of grayish head,
Over the snowy Alps, some wind comes blow her stead.
So what! Then hovering over the wide abyss,
The cloud slowly becomes a gigantic glacier,
And a thousand finials magically would place her
Like a crown to this edifice.

Like the highest of points of a rocky mountain,
Then it stands, at distance, with crest of cold disdain.
The wavering rainbow tickles its flank of steel,
And every night when fall the shadows at its feet,
The sunshine blasting rays turn its snow into sleet
And resurfaces its appeal.

Its heights during the night glare like an eerie dawn,
And the rapid escape that makes the frightened fawn
And the somber eagle all mighty and quiet.
The tempest, at its feet, twists and twirls and then drags.
The eye-reach, any day, to climb its top just lags;
So untroubled it stands as yet.

All alone in these heights, all serene and steady,
My mind forgets all things of this world already,
Sees the day full of star and the sky's true colors,
And contemplates first-class these heavenly splendors
Of the night's gentleness and perpetual candors
Until the first morning pallor

Brings rays from the heavens to change its demeanor,
Then the large icy blocks turn into streams meaner
That run down, roaring loud, on the cold mountain flanks
And go wash, cold and proud in the welcoming sea,
Attempting so vainly, other shores to go see,
Breaking off with the riverbanks.

To the heavenly flow, like so vibrates my mind,
From the blissful circle it never falls behind.
From the earthly ocean with its bitter waters,
Just like with the sunrays rises up a thick smoke,
It rises to the bliss and, always unprovoked,
Comes back much richer thereafter.

Data Fata Secutus

This century toddled! Rome was the new Sparta,
Napoleon slowly used Bonaparte's data,
And from the first consul, in many ways, you'd see,
Piercing the emperor with subtle urgency.

That's when in Besançon, Spanish city of old,
Tossed like a grain of wheat in the air, in the cold,
Was born Breton as well as Lorraine as can be,
A child bereft of tint, of nature, mere freebie,
So feeble that he was, as a true delusion,
Forsaken by the crowd, mother in omission,
With his neck weak and frail, bent up like a willow,
That no one dared invest into his tomorrow.
This child clinging to life, devoid of tooth and nail,
Who, in the thoughts of all, thriving would surely fail,
Tis I.

I will divulge, one of these blessed days,
What good milk and sweet care and prayers sent my way
Were poured into this life, in which I came all damned,
Made me sprout in twofold from my mother hardened
And determined to raise, sweet angel, her three kids
And would pour all her love throughout numerous deeds.

O love of a mother! Love that no one forgets!
Heavenly bread spread out that God only begets!
First tangible display of God's unwavering care,
To everyone given, to all evenly shared!

I can easily say, one of these dubious nights,
When in my golden days, with weak and flickering sight,
I'll narrate how my fate of glory and terror
That troubled the whole world under the emperor,
Amid all the thunder, cradled my weak stature
And bounced me here and there to its fitted measure.
For when the Nor'easter perturbs its still waters,
The sea convulses then and tosses thereafter
The mighty destroyer, with its large guns that roar,
Just like the fallen leaf from any tree, seashore!

Now that I am still young and often put through tests,
I recall much clearly the trials sent to my nest.
And it easily shows how much I underwent
By the forehead furrows that I so rarely vent.
Of course, many elders, with deceived experience,
Having lost every hope in life-ending cadence,

Would shudder if faced up, like a profound abyss,
My soul where all my thoughts reside and never miss
To stir what I suffered and what I tried in vain,
All I was lied about that brought sorrow and pain,

The good time in my life, gone to never return,
The loves, the works, the deaths, all experienced in turn,
And although I'm still young, an age so full of hope,
With pages of my heart where silently I mope.

If at times I disclose of my thoughts, the nature,
And they go all over, quashing my composure,
If it's pleasing to me to put love and sorrow

Deep within a novel, ironic and narrow,
And if my fantasy makes tremble any stage,
If I put in display, to crowds of any age,
Other people like them, living my life somewhat,
Facing people like me, having similar chat,

If my head, true furnace where smolders up my mind,
Spits out strong verses, steaming as I can find,
Deep within a rhythm, as a mysterious frame,
From where stem the stanzas, with wings no one can tame,

It's just that love, the tomb, the life, and the glory,
The ever-running stream by a river, carried,
Every breath, every ray, auspicious or fatal,
Give their glow to my soul of the finest crystal,
My soul so outspoken that the God I adore
Placed in the midst of all, like subtle metaphor.

Besides, I had my share of days heavy laden,
And I know where I'm from although lost in this den.
The tempests of the world with strong winds all stirring,
Without troubling its sea, of my soul caused the swing.
Nothing vile in my heart, no grudge lying dormant,
That would wait for a chance to act some resentment.

After all that I voiced, now I watch, contemplate,
The fallen emperor, honored but not too late,
Treasuring my freedom for all its benefits,
The throne fit for its king, the king, its demerits,
Faithful to the dear blood that was poured in my veins
Of my father, soldier, and mother, Vendéen.

Mazeppa

I

So then when Mazeppa, all roaring and crying,
Saw himself, arms and feet, his flank saber-brushing
All members fastened tight
On a spirited horse, by marine grass nourished,
Running all fired up, fear of speed all vanquished,
Fueled by some unknown spite.

When he, all unfastened, wiggling like a reptile,
Managed, with futile rage, to put a grinning smile
On his dreaded killers,
That he at last saddled this fierce and agile rump,
Overheated, foaming, galloping at full pump,
Like a willing miller.

A cry soared, and right there, dashing through the prairie,
The man and his fierce mount, short of breath, are carried
Right above the quicksand,
Alone, filling the air with a noisy whirlwind,
Like a black cloud stirring and a lightning that spins,
Flew into the air strand.

They race through all the vales like a passing thunder,
Like those mighty tempests the mounts get crushed under,
Like a fiery globe.
Then they just disappear, a black dot in the sky,
And no more trace of them; that's how fast they flew by,
The deep azure to probe.

They've flown into the sky, in the immense azure;
Toward the unending horizon that allures,
They both rush gracefully.
They race like wing-propelled, and the mighty great oaks,
Towns, towers, and mountains by their high speed provoked
Bow down docilely.

If the unfortunate, with his head falling back,
Budges, the horse bounces steadily on his track,
With a bigger startle,
Shoots through the vast desert, arid, impassable,
Spreading infinitely with its folds palpable
Like a hide of cattle.

All waver and appear with a spectrum unknown.
The forest rushes by, and the big clouds have flow.
The old fort went under;
The mountain rays bathing the space between them made
Open up to display cattle speeds unafraid,
Dashing rolling thunder.

And the sky, where the dusk spreads down its veil swiftly,
With its immensity of clouds that willingly
Cling on as they fly by,
And this sunshine piercing at any opening,
All alone on its stage, shines loud in the ceiling,
Golden rays of the sky.

Blinded, it loses track, and its flowing mane drags.
Its head dangles; its blood rushing spills in large bags
        All over the forest.
On its muscles all tight, the band tightens anew
And, like a long serpent, narrows and binds the few
        Knots and bite on its chest.

And the horse all-ablaze, devoid of any sense,
Still bleeding and fleeing, running from some offense,
        His flesh torn on the way,
Alas! To this frantic and trepidant escape
That followed after it, with flowing manes like cape,
        Ravens came in to play.

Ravens, the great horned owl, which to itself is scared,
The great eagle warrior, the goldfishes in pair,
        With their ruby eyelids,
The slanting owls as well, and the tawny vulture
That, through cadaver flanks, ferociously punctures
        Its meals raw and fetid,

They all joined in the flight, this all-forsaken swarm.
They left their world behind, the holm oak near the farm,
        The cozy manor nests.
All distraught and bloody, not perceiving their joy,
It wondered, seeing them, who could've dared deploy
        A swarm with such a zest.

An all-gloomy nightfall, bereft of any star,
Descended on the swarm following not so far,
The traveler steaming.

Right above in the sky, like a somber whirlwind,
He hears and then loses, like a race no one wins,
Their faint flutter of wings.

And then after three days of never-ending race,
After crossing rivers, never losing its trace,
Over deserts and woods,
The horse fell, and all birds gave a sudden uproar,
And with its iron shoes, over stony decor,
Canceled its lightning brood.

There he goes, the wretched, lying there miserably,
Naked and all bloody, with its soul probably
All-ready to depart.
And the birds, flocking high in circle nonending,
Create a swarm of beaks, their descent readying
Like thousand hungry darts.

Well then, this convicted, who's howling and dragging
Its soon-to-become corpse, Ukraine tribe loud bragging
Someday will make him prince.
One day, sowing the fields of their unknown warriors,
It will rightfully grant with feast with no barrier
All vultures and ravens.

Its wild and mighty fame will sprout from its torture.
One day, to old hetmans, it will belt the old fur,
Admiring eyes to see;
And as it marches on, these tent-living people,
Prostate, will all follow of the fanfare ripple
The band musical sea.

II

So then, when a human, in whom his god resides,
Is fastened on your rump, wiggling from side to side,
Master of fiery race,
Alas! In vain he fights. You sprint and carry him
Far away from the world to the well-hidden streams,
Leaving a silver trace.

Along with him, you cross deserts and hoary heights
Of the old mounts, the seas, and there, shaking of fright,
Down the somber valleys.
And all the unclean ghosts, awakened by your thrust,
Around the said rider daringly come adjust
The hordes of their trolleys.

He crosses, in the flight, on your fiery wings,
All the ethereal worlds, all the possible things,
Drinks from the living source.
In the nights of thunder or in the starry night,
His hair mixed with the tails of shooting stars alight
Shines bright along its course.

The six moons of Herschel, the ring of old Saturn,
And the pole sketchy curve when morning light returns
Over the boreal front,
And he sees everything. Your unrelenting flight,
Of this infinite world, pushing the ideal sight,
The horizon affronts.

Who really can figure, spiritual beings aside,
What it takes to keep up and the lightning that rides
Your brightly shining eyes?
Since he will be charred up by such a flamboyance,
Alas! And in the night, who knows his annoyance
When cold wings come chastise?

He cries, all frightened up, but you go on steady.
Pale, weary, and gaping, he caves in already,
Sagging from sheer terror.
Every step that you take seems to open the tomb,
And at the very end, he runs, flies, and succumbs
Then rises emperor!

The Power of Hope

Let's all keep hope alive! All you unfortunate!
Nothing is here to stay, don't go mope over fate,
No hell is forever!
All sorrow goes to God, like arrow to the mark.
All good deeds are hinges holding the strong and stark
Heavenly barrier.

Grieving is a virtue; the remorse is the pole
Of shackled-up monsters whose breath all freedom stole
When we face our Maker.
The livings remain chaste in their carnal casings,
And Death, tender angel, returns back their two wings
To souls who reenter.

The hades will become Eden; it's their duty.
Every globe is a bird endowed with sheer frailty.
And again I utter,
Virtues, among us all, do the majestic task
Of rewarding us with merits, and so we bask
In paradise glitter.

The time is near! Have faith! Come rekindle the soul!
Let's love one another! This is the holy toll
To get to God's alcove.
The somber universe, cold, distant is in need
Of this sublimation, rising away from greed
To the kingdom of love!

Already, the somber ocean God created,
The shadowy islands of jails are elated.
God is the great lover,
And the globes, opening their cold, sinister eyes
Toward the sheer greatness, breaking all sullied ties,
Slowly come and hover.

Oh! How they'll resonate the blessed harmonies,
How blessed they will glow, with all host symphonies,
All those faces of light,
How delighted will be the blessed firmament,
How quivering they'll sound, the harps at this moment
Of love in all its might.

When the earthly monster opening wide its claws
Will melt in sheer splendor all the dread of the laws,
Making honey from gall,
Drowning deep in beauty the night rendered mellow,
Just like the loving sun makes a lovely rainbow
From any cloud it calls,

God with his loving stare, drawing the shadows near,
Seeing merge toward Him, from the cesspool of fear,
Where evil would pray Him,
Rise from the great abyss, stammering with praises,
Will let amid all his archangels He dazes
The prince of evil themes!

And then will palpitate all recanted mires,
And the worst wickedness then will be admired.
In the peak the highest,
The spider glowing bright at sills of pilasters
Will stand up and carry cobs of stars much faster,
As straw for jailhouse nest,

And the brightness will soar in everything as sap.
You'll see glowing the face of the bull in its nap,
The heavenly crescent.
The grave keeper will sing, encumbered in horror,
And over the manure will rise from the terror
A Job gleaming, lucent.

O disappearance of the old anathema!
The depths telling his love to the Heights, the Summa!
Return of the wretched!
What a dazzle therein the all-sublime heavens!
What a surge of brightness, seeing the depths advance,
Uttering, "Be blessed!"

You will see the great herd of the famous hydras
Of inscrutable mists; they'll spring from the abyss
And will be transfigured,
And bright stars will emerge from the holes of their skulls,
Just Lord! And then slowly become luminous balls,
The azure, come figure.

They will come all speechless, powerless, and all mute,
Lost! And bright aureoles will come, as though astute,
Melt the horns of their heads.
They will clasp in their claws, amid the firmament,
Rays that fizzle just as palms of great contentment,
And maws will kiss instead!

They will come! They will come, shaking from ecstasy,
Each one sobbing rivers, sobbing from what they'd see,
But not a bit of fright.
They will be all welcome in peaceful paradise,
And Jesus, while lining to Belial in loud sighs,
Will say, "Come to the light!"

And to God, hand in hand, He will take His brother!
And when they'll be walking, one next to the other
For blessed eyes to see,
They will be so glorious that God, with probing sight,
Will stand to realize, Father filled with delight,
The fruit of His mercy!

All will be said. Evil will come to end, the tears
Will dry up, no more prongs, no more death, no more fears.
The infamous abyss,
While losing all its depths, will stutter, "I am here!"
Sorrow will be no more, in the skies, loud and clear,
Will ring, "Let's start the bliss!"

May Madness

The brightness all around my soul does not trouble.
Like a lovely maiden, the fields shine and bubble;
The nest dangles in the hollies.
Gaiety glows everywhere, and the world gladly raves.
May, in the moss, spreading, deep within every cave
To the lovebirds shows sweet follies.

In fields of alfalfa as in the fields of beans,
Frolicking butterflies dance like in dreaming scenes,
The green corn sprouts from rugged stalls,
And golden bees hover periwinkle branches.
The thyme and the bindweed, growing on the ranches,
Let all these suckers have a ball.

The eventide displays copper clouds in the sky.
The trees bursting with leaves on spring seem to be high,
Throwing their branches without care;
Birds are tossed over here and again are flung there.
The braided drone comes flirt with roses everywhere,
Sweet nothings only it would dare.

I let rise in the air the balms and all the scents,
Let the flowers whisper, like ghosts in shady tents.
And when morning dawns, they all flee!
Taking my time, alone I subtly introspect,
Ponder over the scenes of my somber aspect,
Think about the dead, the ones free!

For before you know it, before long, O my love,
Before the flow returns, I'll come to you, my dove,
One day of spring, of month of May,
Under some shady turf, under a bursting tree.
From all this sweet madness, I'll be finally free,
In my cold tomb with no dismay.

Avarice and Envy

Avarice and Envy, strolling freely one day,
Toward the fields, were on their way,
Over a bad man or a nut,
At yours or at someone else's or over my house... but then
No one knew their target, but
They went like they'd lost their den.

Though sisters, these two monsters
Hate each other, so at every step of the way,
Without a sound, they went on no faster.
Avarice hunched back as she stays,
Admiring this most precious coffer
For which constantly she surveyed;
Envy as well kept snooping at the prey.

Counting all the gold coins that in the chest glittered,
Along the trail, dame Avarice
Kept repeating to herself this:
"I don't have enough!" she uttered.
Meanwhile, Envy, peering with sneaky glance,
Lurking this gold so precious to her eyes,
Would say, twisting her mouth in trance,
"She has too much. Less is my size!"

Each one, in her own way, reflected on the chest.
Then Desire came to the test,
Desire, this strong god, able to satisfy
Just every wish sent to her with loud sighs.

Desire then said, "Ladies,
I am gallant, and you, missies,
Come then and choose whatever you so please,
Treasure, honor, and what you seize.

"Before all, let's get something clear:
The first one who utters a sound
Will get her wish, all safe and sound.
The second gets double the cheers."
You can see in what kind of jam
This deal put the two go-getters.
Misers and envious, what's now to do? Goddamn!
Each one within herself mumbled to the quidam,
"What's to me, O Desire, your treasures, your glitters?
What are to me these goods set up with conditions
If others top my possessions?"

And both, with this disastrous trick,
Hesitated with no reason.
Desire, god agile and quick,
Curses and swears and in the thick,
Hell, to them, offers as prison.
Cruel and implacable, Envy then suddenly
Looked at her sister, while growling,
Then, right away, self-deciding,
Yelled, "Take off one of my eyes only!"

The Last Free Meal

When the old Olympus, the Word to immolate,
Weighing on decision of Roman magistrate,
From some wretched temple,
Furiously would condemn Christians all elated,
Victims of wild tigers, beasts well agitated,
To gods give as sample,

Rome offered a last meal to the elected saints,
As though in the chalice filled up with crude absinthe
They'd pour drops of honey.
He pitied the martyrs but ignored their transport.
He wanted to appease by an act of some sort
All those from Bethany.

The purple would welcome their many austere guests.
Falernum was foaming in craters, poured with zest,
By cute myrtles girdled.
The honey of Hybla tinted the Malmsey wine,
And in golden vessels, their feet with scented pine
Were washed although boggled.

A solemn force, mixing the tribes of the three worlds,
Depleted the forests, and the sea fruits unfurled
For this free-of-charge meal.
You'd say that by drawing lavishly from nature,
Sybaris invited to feast of Epicure
The ones Charon would steal.

Meanwhile, the tigers pulled violently on their chain;
The leopards, still in cage, crazily searched in vain
The arena's exit.
But soon much less cruel than the ladies of Rome,
Those beasts would be stunned by the delight from the dome
Seeing what they would eat.

They'd throw to the lions, confessors, even priests.
Like a servant that feeds, masters he can't resist,
Favorite meals of their choice.
Yet at the pompous feast would assist their conclave,
Livid of fright, standing, just like a deaf-mute slave
Would hear die down their voice.

II

O kings, your lives will end, like finishes a meal.
The cup of majesty sought by the common still
Shines, clung within your fist,
But a joyous concert of this much-transient feast
Is lost within the growls of the popular beast
That has you on its list.

The End

I

Of a given nation, one day I scanned the past!
Fatal accounts of death, of might that did once last.
That's when I felt shiver my lute of modern days.
Every time I'd read of a great crime, a great name,
Which one or the other would rise high up in fame,
It would, back with time, fade away.

Let's shut it up for now, this formidable book.
Stop interrogating this unreachable spook
Who remains there silent, half monster and half god.
The riddle it presents eludes many lyres.
It only writes its themes on conquered empires
With letters of fire and blood.

II

Let's not look for this word. Then tell me why, you poet,
That you stay wide-awake, with your lyre upset?
Why expose her to this and thus sell her for short?
Why your sinister chant and your meaningless voice?
I just needed, good taste of choice,
A mighty nation to exhort.

Of forsaken revolts I'd peer in the abyss?
But you need sheer chaos if you pursue justice.
In the dead of my night, to me it was uttered.
I meant to, by leading the crowd to the mission,
Before this era's conclusion,
Tackle the era that ended.

The genius is in need of a nation that sets
His soul bright aflame till his own self he forgets.
A whole generation is what he needs to rule.
And once he takes his flight off this high mountain ridge,
He needs not rest on any bridge;
The whole ocean is his footstool!

That's where he spreads his wings, right where he freely roars,
And over deep waters, to the blue sky he soars.
That is where he can bounce as whimsical giant,
Spin and twirl as fancied in the raging tempest,
Riding waterspouts at their best,
One arm holding the firmament.

Sorrow of Olympio

The fields were not somber, and the sky, not dreary.
No, their day was beaming, favoring a fairy
Of the clearest azure,
The air filled with fragrance, the fields all fresh and green
When he revisited this place where he had been
Through such grieving torture!

The autumn all-aglow, the hills toward the plain
Would slope their wood foliage whose green could not remain
Under this golden sky,
And the birds, to the Source of everything that's good,
Would sing in unison, giving thanks for the food
They receive from on high!

He wanted to see all again in its wholeness
The pond nearing the brook, the hovel that God blest,
And the old bent-up oak,
The love resorts hidden so well deep in the woods,
The tree where the kisses, their blessings to prelude,
Airs of bliss had provoked!

He searched for the garden, the isolated house,
The fence, then the alley leading the eyes to douse
Into banks of orchard.
Pale, he walked to the sound of his somber footsteps,
And at every tree seen, pale shadows came and leapt,
To his heart's disregard!

He caught the shuddering from the forest he loves,
This sweet breeze that triggers, when it comes gently shove,
Love's most precious recalls,
And shaking the old oak or swinging the red rose,
It seemed like the great Soul, coming down just to pose,
Would, at turn, on all fall.

The dead leaves on the soil of the lonely forest,
Seemingly rising up, his steps to come attest,
Would run in the garden.
Just like the wounded soul, would tell the thoughts to fly,
A short flight to fall back with their soft, silent sighs,
As though heartache laden.

Then he contemplated for long the awesome forms
That takes Mother Nature under peaceful plain norms;
He daydreamed till the night.
Every day he wandered up and down the gully,
Admiring, in turn, the azure, clear, jolly,
The lake mirrors aright!

Alas! By recalling his treasured adventures,
Peering, not entering, over the green closures,
Just like an outcast,
He wandered all day long. Then the night's somber womb
Rendered his heart so sad, as sad as a cold tomb;
Therefore, he said in blast,

"O sorrow! I wanted, laden with troubled soul,
To taste and see if the urn had some of its stock,
And see if this sweet vale had prepared as a dole
Some that my broken heart had once left here in shock.

"So little is needed for time to change so much!
O you, serene nature, how easy you forget!
And since you change all things, how easy you come touch
The mysterious bonds that the sweethearts target!

"Our foliage quarters have turned into thickets,
The tree marked of our names is dead or left toppled,
Our roses are all dead, which were in the pen set,
By all the running kids that jumped, all so supple.

"A wall girds the fountain where, when it'd get too warm,
Friskily she would drink, coming down from the woods.
She would take the water in her hands with such charm
And let the pearls drip down as gently as she could.

"They paved the rough roadway that was so uneven,
Where in the virgin sand would imprint properly
With such blunt irony, she was so small, given,
Her footstep that appeared next to mine so lovely!

"The roadside, which was built, given such a long time,
Where she'd come and sit down until I would arrive
Is all gone from hitting, mostly in the nighttime,
The big tractor-trailers that their way back would drive.

"Here there's no more forest. There it spreads in the fields.
Of all that we cherished, nothing is left standing.
And just like cold ashes that the time failed to shield,
The load of souvenirs scatters by wind blowing!

Did not we exist once? Are we lost back in time?
Will we ever come back as cherished memory?
The breeze strokes the tree branch, but I hear somber chime.
And to my own dwelling, I'm just transitory.

"Others will come trample the same pathway we trailed.
Once it was you and I, but then others will come.
And the dream we dreamed of, in which we poorly failed,
They will come and attempt but with bleak outcome!

"For no one in this world gets to really complete.
We never reach the end despite all our efforts.
We will always wake up right where happiness splits.
All starts in one world but ends in distant resorts.

Yes, others will, in turn, come down, candid couples,
Draw from this lovely place, so peaceful and charming,
Everything that nature, to love often muffled,
Fills up with reverie and all solemn bearings!

"Others will claim our fields, our trails, our hiding spots.
Your forest, my sweet dove, belongs to some unknown.
Other ladies will come and fight the waves you fought
And erase the footprints you left on the green lawn!

"So what! It is in vain that here, in love we fell!
We will not guard a thing from these flowery hills
Where we became just one, all caught up in the spell!
Nature, stolid and cold, came and all from us steal.

"Oh, tell me, you gullies, running brook, ripe grapevine,
Branches of nests laden, caves, forests, and bushels,
Will you in other ears, your sweet murmurs, define?
Will you sing your sweet songs that just the heart retells?

"We were so attentive, so austere, so enthralled!
We had a sweet accord with all echoes around!
And we remained so keen not to trouble at all
The least of the babbles from your numerous sounds.

"Answer then, clear valley, answer, you solitude,
O nature all abloom in this lovely desert,
When we will fall asleep, bearing the attitude
That gives to those dreaming an aspect so inert,

"Will you choose to remain so cold in demeanor,
Knowing so well we're here, having lost all our love,
While you keep your fiesta, nothing can be meaner,
While you still smile away, singing like turtledove?

"Is it that seeing us wandering your precious nooks,
Phantoms recognized by your mounts and your forests,
You would choose to retain the secrets we once took,
Those that you could reveal to old friends out of zest?

"Will you stand there, seeing, and utter no complaint,
Our shadows wander where we once lively trod,
And watch her drag my heart, in a cheerless restraint,
Toward some weeping brook with sad tears in a pod?

"And if in some corner, where all is calm, somber,
Two lovebirds come display their love to your flowers,
Would you not go tell them so they can remember,
'Hey you two, full of zest, think of the sad hours!'

"God allows for a while that we use His nature;
The shivering forests, the rocks heavy and mute,
And the peaceful azure, the lakes, and the pastures
To cradle loving hearts, their dreams and their pursuits!

"Then He takes it away. He blows off the candle,
Putting us in the dark while we thought we saw light,
And commands to the fields, where we had first kindled,
To erase our footsteps and to forget our sight.

"Well then! Forget us all, house, garden, shadow!
Grass, come grow all over. Bramble, cover our trace!
Birds, sing your tunes. Brooks, keep rolling. All foliage, grow!
The ones that you forget will remember your face.

"For you'll remain for us the real faces of love!
You are the oasis upon this desert road!
You are the quiet vale, the halcyon alcove
Where we shed many tears, hand in hand, painful load!

"Every given passion over time away fades.
One erases its mask, and the other, its knife,
Like a group of actors in some happy parade
Touring from town to town on the stage of one's life.

"But, love, you never fade. You always stir our hearts!
You who, torch or beacon, shines aglow in our fog!
You hold us all captives with the mirth you impart.
The youth repudiates you. The old upholds your blog.

"In this golden of age, of years gravely laden,
When we drag aimlessly, bereft of true vision,
The self, pure reflection of an old lion's den,
Where repose all our dreams and all our illusions,

"When the soul penetrates the depths of our entrails,
Scoping deep in the heart that the shiver invades,
Just like you scope the dead upon a fierce war trail,
Every fallen sorrow, every dream, lifeless laid,

"Just like someone searching, holding high a weak torch,
Far from the real objects, far from the world laughter,
She slowly steps to get to this dark sloping porch
To reach the dreary end of the inner chapter.

"And then in this dark room that not a star comes shine,
The soul takes a step back from where all seems to end
But notices something in some veil intertwined …
-Ah! That's you sleeping there, Souvenir, my dear friend!"

The Past

Twas a mighty castle, back from Louis the Thirteenth;
The setting sun inflamed this forgotten palace.
Every window glowing, in furnace blazing scenes,
Seemed to be lost amid this giant ember screen
As the roof disappeared like by sunrays erased.

In front of us, fallen, glory of days of old,
One of these parks with grass spread all over the trail,
At the corner, standing, on gray base, looking cold,
Halfway ivy covered, attracting frogs too bold,
A statue is warmed up by fire, caught in hail.

Sadly, a great pond lies, as solitary lake.
A large greenish Neptune molded in the water.
The reeds hid the dark pool that slowly the ground slaked.
And the trees would mingle, as though to overtake
This spot where in the past, Boileau's rhymes did matter.

And every now and then, roaming in the forest,
You'd see majestic deers bored and missing hunters,
And lonely white marbles, with tree trunk in contest.
Under the thick foliage, changing their frozen zest,
Gabrielle and Venus stood, these statue sisters.

The hoisted overcoats by the worn rapier,
Alas! No longer walked through this muttered garden.
The tritons seemed to be somewhat so happier,
And lost in the shadows, not a bit lazier,
Yawning deep in the woods, gapes widely an old den.

And then I tell you this: This castle in the dark
Has harbored as much love as glowing in your heart,
With glory and laughter along with feasts with mark,
And all this past gaiety today renders it stark,
Just like a stained vessel by liquor much too tart.

In this den where the moss spreads all over the grain,
Would step in hesitant yet with stampeding breast
Either the sweet Caussade or the Candale maiden,
Who, of a royal prince being the feudal gain,
Coming in, would say, "Sir", but "Charles," leaving the nest.

But then since nowadays, for Candale or Caussade,
The thick brume golden fluff redressing the azure,
The feeble rays gilding the roof's somber facade,
The windows lively blazed, as fiery cascade,
And the sun was pleasant in this fairy nature,

But then since nowadays, two sweethearts or two souls
Wandered under this green where much love was display';
He declared his duchess an angel to behold,
And with eyes all aglow by sweet love rendered bold,
They'd inflame the other since it is nowadays!

Somewhere deep in the woods, you'd hear candid laughter
Just another couple lost in their private bliss.
At time, a short instant would cause them to falter.
Gently he would ask her, "Why did you sigh after?"
Supple, she would reply, "Why did you ask me this?"

Both the king, the angel, tenderly, hand in hand,
Would walk, proud and happy, upon the mushy grass,
Blending their sights, their breaths, and every thought at hand...
O the sweet good old days! O shrouded splendid land!
O sunrays now swallowed by this somber compass!

At the Feuillantines circa 1813

Children, cute and naive, all around me swarming,
Bright shining enamel, questioning everything.
You, always inquiring on important problems,
You want of all aspects, as somber as they stem,
To discover the sense and the precise meaning
That tackles every thought in my mind daydreaming
So much that when you leave, children, often I glide
For long hours, painful to replace in their slide,

Deep down in my thinker, my plans and my visions,
My unending subjects of my meditations:
God, man and the future, the reason, dementia.
My systems, somber pile, despite the inertia,
Perturbed so suddenly, with no fault of your own,
By childish inquiries so haphazardly thrown!
Since you are all around weighing my tomorrow,
That you are so eager to dig deep and burrow
Into my early gifts and my early impulse,
Listen then, my dear friends, your plea I won't repulse!

I had, in my childhood, alas! That went too fast
Three masters: a garden, an old priest, and the last,
My mother. The garden large, deep, and mysterious,
Enclosed by tall ramparts erected so curious,
With flowers all dispersed, like beautiful eyelids,
With all shades of insects running chores so rapid

Its stones, buzzing their ways in sounds ever muttered,
In the middle, behind, a field with trees scattered.
The old priest, well imbued of Tacit and Homer,
Was a humble old man. Mother, she was my mère!

That's how I developed, molded by these three heads.
One day if Gauthier would care to lend me his lead,
I would depict to you what I want to instill
That one day at the house, came in, oh! Somber feel!
A doctor looking poor, solemn in poise and age,
I would certainly see, from your lips free of rage,
The doors of your young hearts, harboring no worry,
Burst in candid laughter, the kind that won't scurry!

And when this man came in, I was in the garden.
As soon as I saw him, I stopped all a sudden.

He was the principal of some unknown college.
The tritons of Coypel misguided in their pledge!
The wildlife that Watteau deep in the woods misled,
Sorcerers of Rembrandt, the fairies Goya led,
The disparate devils of any monk's nightmare,
With which laughing Callot would St. Antony dare,
Are ugly yet charming, misshapen yet brightened
By a fire by which their faces are gladdened,
And at times from their eyes burst lightning so rapid.
Our man was so ugly, was as well as stupid.

My bad, I speak of this like the average schoolkid.
It's bad. What I said came as from a rotten seed!
For at a happy stage that a pedant disturbs,
I still kept the anger; my grace went to the curb.

This bald and somber man, to me all too scary
For whom mother as well some fright had once carried,
As he generated all humble attitudes,
Would offer advices and his solicitudes
That the child was not geared and that also, at times,
He would carry his books to the woods citing rhymes
That at times he'd meet him, bathing in solitude.
We should think of the goal, a stern study preludes,
The setting of a room with deep dour cloisters,
Lit by just one old lamp in the ceiling hoisted,
For a hundred students writing keen and agile
That gave light to Horace, Catullus, and Virgil
Would do so much better to the fermenting mind
Than the branches of trees through which sunrays come shine
And that it was needed that children left mothers
For the yoke, hard labor, and such useful bothers.

Therefore, the stern college; triumphant, nurturing,
With calming atmosphere, offers to the young teen,
Yearning for liberty, fresh air, joy, and roses,
Its benches of black oak, its dorms time imposes,
Its classrooms that they lock with their many pillars
That with nails often sculpt the young and bored scholars,
Its teachers who assure, amid of paperwork,
The thorough completion of sanction dreary work,
And free of water, lawn, trees, and the many fruits,

Its large playground all paved, suited for kid pursuits.

The man, through and dismissed, left all flabbergasted,
My mother who sat down, sad and disconcerted.
What to do? What to think? What was the best action?
Or the dreary college or the pleasant mansion?
Who best know, of this life, how to deal with punches,
The troublesome schoolboy or the child who trenches?

Problems! Heavy questions! She wavered painfully.
The decision had heft. Hapless lady truly,
Molded from destiny, not scholarly produced,
How to face up the charge of this wretched magus,
With his masterful voice and his woeful gestures
Talking about the Greek and Latin great statures?
The priest was a scholar, with no doubt, but then hey,
Do you learn from teachers or how a college sways?

And then more than often this is how we conquer!
The man the most vulgar needs his own debunker:
"It's indispensable, it's fitted, and matters!"
These often unbalance the most poised of "maters."
Poor mother! Which way then to follow? What to choose?
The whole fate of her son depended on her snooze.
Trembling she so remained, weighing these two options,
And at times it would seem to give her attention
To the college, alas! Pitting in face-to-face
My current happiness or the one at my chase.

And she pondered this way, with no sleep and no break.

'Twas in summer, the time when the earth, the moon stakes.

One of these warm evening vaguely favoring day,
Not as bright but loaded with kindness on its sleigh,
In her park where would play moon rays lulled by the breeze,
She wandered yet saddened, still with noted unease,
Questioning all inside, water, heaven, forest,
Keenly searching for some reply to her request.

That's at these cool hours that the peaceful garden,
The undergrowth shudders by some insect hidden,
The beetle rocked steady by the leaves, the lizard
Running in the moonlight, shunning human regards,
The earthenware blue leaves from which shape the plant takes,
The eastern cupola of somber Val-de-Grâce,
The cloister of convent, broken and yet tranquil,
The chestnut trees, the green alley somber appeal,
The statue upon which brush every branch shadow,
The pale bindweeds, the white daisies in subtle row,
All the many flowers of the bush, trees, and reeds
Giving back as sweet tune, their essence steady feed,
Mirroring in the pond or hiding in the grass,
Or which, the ebony suffering their weak pass,

Around the limpid ponds, along with the birch tree,
Tremble in golden grapes in the grooves that you see
And the sky glimmering behind the thick foliage,
And the rooftops spreading the smoke, leaving its cage,
That's at these times of bliss, as I was telling you,
That this precious garden, small Eden made anew,

The old crumbling stone wall, all the many roses,
These thought-provoking themes, all nature's sweet doses,
Murmured to my mother, with waves and breezy fuss,
And said to her frankly, "Please leave this child with us!

Oh, leave the child with us, poor and baffled mother!
With his keen, candid sight whose shine can't be smothered,
This soul so far untouched by any mourning veil,
This genuine true spirit, Mother, please do not fail!
Do not haphazardly throw him into the crowd
That always crushes those caught deep into its shroud.
Just like the little birds, all kids have inner fright.
Allow to the fresh air and to the steamy sights,
To the whispering sighs, as light as wings of dream,
This ever-solemn mouth that never lays a scream
And this bright naive smile enrobed in sheer candor!
O mother full of love, let your child get tender!

We promise to give him only most worthy thoughts.
We'll turn into bright days the pale shades that he brought.
God will come visible to his delighted eyes,
For we are the flowers, the branches that disguise.
We dress Mother Nature. We're the unending source
Where every thirst is quenched, we're every mind's recourse.
And the fields, the forest that only wise men fill,
Teach every great spirit how to see and to feel.
Allow the child to grow among our solemn sounds.
We will instill in him every essence around,
Kindled by heaven's breath and spread over the earth
That springs from every man ascending from its girth,

Reaches up to the Lord, like a hymn or incense,
Every hope, precious love, all prayers, and sweet trance!
We'll call his attention on the shadows at hand
To every known secret that he tries to attend.
From this child we will make a man, then a poet.
To shape of his senses the bud frail and upset,
You will have to choose us, and we'll unveil to him
How from the dusk to dawn, from oaks to smallest themes,
Being in all, reflects, colors, vapors, all lives,
Life in every aspect chuckles in fields and thrives.
He will be down-to-earth and of heaven dazzled,
And we'll allow growing every thought that frazzles
For the humans, all lost, sadly under so much,
This pity that springs out, admiring nature's brush!
Give us this lovely child, and we'll give him a heart
That understands women; a spirit that won't thwart,
From where will easily bud dreams and delusions
That will follow closely the good Lord's instructions;
A soul, candid source of the most secret favors,
That will shine pleasantly for dreamers to savor
And, just like the warm sun over fertile flowers,
Will shed the light of his thought-provoking power!"

That's the way it was said at the end of the day
By stars and plants and trees, and my mother obeyed.

Children! Did they uphold their part of the bargain?
I don't know. But I know that my mother had gained
Insight and followed them, saving my soul from jail,
Entrusted my young soul to tread upon their trails.

From then, before the night, time chosen to study,
Would recall my thinking to be grave and sturdy,
All day long, free, happy, alone under God's dome
I could wander at ease in this garden, my home,

Contemplating all fruits, running water or pond,
The bright and shiny star, the flower that burgeoned,
And the fields, the forests, that at the end of day
Would see back in Virgil as though clearly portrayed.

Children! Love the meadows, the vales, and the fountains,
The pathways where your ears, the nightlife entertains,
The brook and the furrow, flank that never snoozes,
Where come and dwell all thoughts from which one so chooses.
Take yourself by the hand and walk upon the grass,
Observe those who gladly the golden sheaves amass,
Spell throughout the azure, filled with blazing letters,
And when any bird sings, capture God's voice better.

Life going up against all opposite passions
Waits for you, but be good, be true in unison
Against this dreary world that corrupts the weak mind.
Read from the same great book, sharing the joy you'd find,
And just never forget that the meek chosen soul
Created for the light, for poetry as a whole,
That the hearts where God placed, as a serious thought well,
For all noise that triggers some mystery as well,
In a scream, in a sound, or in a vague murmur,
Perceive subtle guidance straight from Mother Nature.

The Nightmare

Over me, all gasping, panting, with head inclined,
He came this night again, you know; and then he sat,
Putting his heavy hand over my soul, confined,
Reveal her in the dark, like a flower all pined,
To the ghosts and their flying bats.

This monster, to the world, takes various striking forms.
Either of a clear lake, with his face of azure,
Or he bursts in laughter in sparkles of red storm.
His eyes are bright lightning; his wings, ablaze, perform
As he swoops on the flaming lure.

Just like impure mirrors, fleeting shades of darkness
Reflect his images in circles around him.
And his face disappears, caught in the steamy mess.
And he disrupts the sleep with waves of fretfulness,
Leaving the soul in dreary dreams.

Virgin! Your peaceful rest is not horror laden.
The night ever lightly treads over your aspect.
Never any bad dream will trouble you, maiden,
For when your soul ascends, at night searching God's den,
Your sleep, a good angel directs.

The Morning

The morning veil glissades over mounts and valleys.
See this ray joyfully brightening the tower,
And in the clear azure, kindled by love power,
From its glory to joy follies,
Rise the first forest tunes to strike every glower.

Come and smile at the glare decorating the dome!
You will see, if ever, the tomb becomes my home.
A sun shines just as bright in your brown teary eyes.
And the same birds solo and the same dawn comes roam
On the pit where my body lies!

Dawning to entity, the soul gladly awakes.
To the infinite being is revealed the true life,
First glow of a span with no strife.
One wakes up from this earthly break
As though from a deep night of nightmare prongs so rife!

Sad Remembrance
(The Street Lad)

The poor child had received two gunshots in the head.
The dwelling was humble, clean, and peaceful instead.
There were a blessed palm hanging on a picture
And an older lady crying with no measure.
We all helped undress him in silence. And his face
Hanging and mouth gaping show death's sneaky embrace,
His arms on either side seemingly needing rest;
A top in his pocket was all he could attest.

In his wound-bleeding hole, one could put a finger.
Have you seen berries bleed on hedge where they linger?
His cranium was open just like a wood gone mad.
The older lady watched as they undress the lad,
Saying, "He is so pale! Come, we need light ample.
God! See how his hair is so stuck to his temple!"
And when it was over, she took him on her knees.
The lugubrious night every echo would seize
Of gunshots in the street from the firing troop.
"We'll have to bury him," advised one of our group.

And they brought a white sheet from the wooden wardrobe
While the grandma took him to the hearth, in white robe,
As though to warm a tad his cold-riddled body.
Alas! Whatever death embraces already
Can no longer be warmed in the hearth of this earth!
She chose to put her arms cuddly around his girth,

Rocking ever gently his precious cadaver.
"Is not it such a sight to make your heart quiver!"
She bellowed! "And, mister, he was not even eight!
His teachers, for he was in school, in him had faith.
Mister, whenever I had to write a letter,
It was he the writer. Now it's a new chapter.

"They're killing the kids now. Now tell me, O dear Lord!
Now we all turn muggers! What a wretched discord!
This very same morning, he was running around!
And now they killed my child. He no more makes a sound!
He was walking the street. They coldly gunned him down.
Mister, he was so good, never gave any frown.
I am an old lady. It's fit that I depart.
That would not change the plans of Mr. Bonaparte,
To kill me in his stead and save this precious life!"

And she stopped for a while; the room, of tears was rife.
Then she said, as they all cried in each other's hold,
"What will become of me, as kin he was my sole?
Please, explain this to me, dear folks of nowadays.
He was the only one left of his mother's lay.
Why did they kill my child? They have to tell me why.
They will have to answer to the powers on high."
We were silent, standing, hats off, serious, somber,
Trembling at this mourning I still can remember.

You will not get a grasp, Mother, of politics.
Mr. Napoleon, that's his name, authentic,
Is poor, but as a prince, he loves the palaces.
He enjoys the horses, the servants, the laces,
His treasure for his game, his table, his alcove,
His hunt parties; and then at the same time, he loves
Family, church, as well as his society.
He wants to have Saint-Cloud, full of floral gaiety,
Where would come at his feet, mayors and magistrates.
That the reason he wants that every grandma's fate,
With their cold, sore fingers that the time has withered,
Be to sew in dark shroud, their kids he has slaughtered.

Someone

So there once was a man, and his name was Varron.
Another Paul-Emile and a third, Cicerone
And they were once great men, powerful, popular;
And they walked, introduced by beams so consular.
They have been generals, magistrates, and speakers
Who have greatly spoken in front of senators.
They witnessed, all amid the great squirming armies,
The flow ever thrilling of eagle drones, steamy.

The crowd would follow them with incessant applause.
They're now dead; they then made to those men of great cause
Majestic marble tombs as well in history.
Their busts are nowadays as grave as their glory,
In the palace's great halls, with eyes vaguely open,
Dream on all around us, spying on all our pain.
But this never hinders us, from other era,
That whenever we speak, recalling their aura,
We say that, on such day, Varron was but a lout,
Paul-Emile had done wrong, Cicerone had no clout."

And when we speak this way of these famous figures,
You rascal, you pretend, cad of a brute nature,
That I talk about you that bores even disdain,
Not saying right out front he is a rascal then!
You'd like that we put on soft gloves and pink mittens
With you who can perturb Sparta, even Athens!
Lots of folks knew of you back in time when you'd run

The poker, the hades, the holes, or the well spun,
When in the night they'd see, either in dark corners,
Or in the dark doorway, with door ajar, loner,
From a den from which spews a somber light-red glow,
Your head wearing, as you come peer, a felt rainbow.

You made yourself garnished by the bohemian king.
Your life is a big joke, down in a poem, wiggling.
And I, what do I care, thinker, judge, or worker,
That December, holding February in choker,
Comes place in some palace you who could soil a hole!
From Vanves to Montrouge, where French carpets are sold,
Run to garrets or caves, in slums where they commune,
You will hear all over resounding the same tune,
"This joke was a big thief. Now he turned minister."
Ah! You want me to hush, imbecile sinister!

Ah! Now you're all happy, satisfied, and smiling!
Don't worry. I will go throughout the town yelling,
"Citizens! Do you see this green-eyed Jesuit?
He used to be Brutus, had all thrones in pursuit,
But he favors them now. He would do anything.
He just wants to succeed. So away with all bling,
But long live the emperor! Away with politics!
He despises Chambord, but Bonaparte, he leaks.
They made him senator. He's now all-fiery.
If things were as they should, this beggar so hungry,
Who has not, as he said, declaiming his posture,
In his heart, the lilies, would shoulder them, for sure!

Last Words

The human conscience died amid some cheap orgy
That over it, crouches, satisfied of this corps;
At times, happy winner, blushing though yet dingy,
She comes back, slaps its face, all devoid of remorse.

The judge prostitution is primary resource.
And the priests nauseate, the puzzled honest man
Down in the potter's field, to the coins they recourse.
Sibour sells back the God Judas once out did hand.

They say, "Long live Caesar, and God the Almighty
Elected him, Himself. People, all bend the knee."
And while they go singing, closing their hands tightly,
You see golden sequins in the palms of many.

Oh! As long as we'll see this wretched prince ruler,
Blessed by the pope still, mischievous potentate,
In one hand the pliers, the other, the scepter,
Charlemagne chiseled down by Satan, not too late;

As long as he wallows, between his teeth crushing
The oath and the virtue, the religious honor,
Drunk and dreadful, its shame on our glory spewing,
The heavens will witness with passive demeanor,

Even if the people abject were to pretend
To come to venerate this abhorrent cheater
And if America or even if England
Would say to the exiled, "Go away, defector!"

Even if we would be of no significance
Or if to please Caesar, they would disown us all,
If the outcast would run through any old entrance
To the crowd torn, haggard, like an old rag of stall,

When the desert where God put His own to the test
Would banish outcasts, chase away the hunted,
Even if infamous or coward like the rest,
The tomb will all expel the bodies of defunct,

I will never back down! Won't utter any sound.
Calm, bearing my mourning, ignoring the others,
I will sternly embrace while I am exile-bound
My country, my freedom that I won't let slaughter!

My noble companions, I keep you in my mind;
Outcasts, the Republic is alive among us.
I'll uphold everything they insult that I find,
And I'll throw my reproach to what they see as just!

I'll remain covered up by sackcloth of ashes,
The voice saying, "Woe!" But that still utters a no.
Meanwhile, your servants clean at the Louvre your trashes.
Your hut I will reveal to you, covered with snow.

Facing all the treason and the salutations,
I will cross both my arms, indignant but serene.
Persistent adherence for the treasured nation,
Be my strength and my joy, the post on which I lean!

Yes, as long as he's there, cause of all this turmoil,
O France, O France, my love, my everyday concern,
I will never step on your sweet and tender soil,
Tomb of my ancestors, nest for the ones I yearn!

I will no longer see your cool and sandy shore,
France! Except for duty, alas! I'll forget all.
Amid the proven ones, I'll remain as before,
Outcast as always for daring to stand tall.

I take the harsh exile, short-term or forever,
Not giving it a thought, with no hesitation
If anyone gave in who should have said "Never"
And if many have left who should remain mentioned.

If we are a large bunch, I'll be right in their midst;
If they are one hundred, then the show must go on.
If only ten remain, I'll be right on the list;
And if there's only one, then I'll say, "Good, come on!"

My Daughter

O my sweet child, you see, I do submit.
Do as I do, live in the world, removed.
Happy? Nope. A winner? Ceding defeat.
Truly soothed!

Be kind and sweet and show a pious stance.
As the day in the sky comes shed its light,
You, my dear child, through blessed forbearance,
Show yours bright!

No one's happy, and no one's a winner.
Time's for us all but remains incomplete.
It's so fleeting and for every sinner
Brings defeat.

Every living pants from under their fate.
To be happy, to all, bleak destiny!
All is missing. Alas! I truly state,
Not many.

This not many is somewhat everyone
In the whole world; we all seek and desire
A word, a name, some money, the true one
You admire!

The king will pine, lifeless, of love deprived.
The desert will lie scorched with no water.
To get his mirth, man never stops to thrive
And batter.

See those wise men that we all idolize,
See those heroes, the so famously known,
All the great names that the world, mesmerize,
Put on throne!

After having in this world brightly shone,
Dazzled by the brightness of their beacon,
They left the scene with a last subtle groan
And flew on.

Heaven, aware of all sorrow and woes,
Always pity our vain and boastful noise.
Every morning the dew to earth it throws
To rejoice.

God leads us on every step of the way
To what to do and what we should desist.
Deep in all hearts He silently conveys,
"Laws exist!"

To His great law, truly we should obey.
It's so unique though so often trampled.
Shun any hate, my child. Love all the way;
It's simple!

To a Mother of a Dead Child

Many times you may say to the poor little child
That all the angels wait for him,
That there he'll be happy, that all is warm and mild,
That you heard their impatient screams,

That under the blue dome with its majestic walls
There's a big tent with bright colors
And a large blue garden with shiny stars in stalls
That have never lost their pallor,

That you can't find the words to say how good it is
To be by angels surrounded,
That you get to play with the cherubs in their bliss,
That you see God, all astounded,

That it is so thrilling to live in fiery love,
Enjoying all eternity
Around the child Jesus in the divine alcove
Of the Virgin of chastity!

You'll never say enough, never, O poor mother,
To this child so feeble and weak,
That he was all you have in this life that smothers
His breath, leaving you cold and bleak.

That when you're small and weak, the mother's love protects.
Later, in turn, we shield her days,
That she will have need of, battling old-age defects,
A grown-up child of her own lay.

You won't have said enough to this young tender soul
That God wants us to live our life,
Woman guiding her man while the latter consoles
Her in her sorrow and her strife.

So that one day, O dear! Inevitable lost,
The dear child from her departed,
As though for having left her birdcage free of post
Your little bird from it parted!

To Mademoiselle L.B.

The years come as they go down this long train of life.
There you see, one ended! And time slowly goes on,
Still another station loaded with its own strife!
Still another winter for the spring to prey on!

The time, the day, the hours, and the words crowd ignores!
Precious words that to her, other cheap words, define!
But when time suddenly, with loud voice, comes and soars,
So few of us mortals take heed to every line.

Man uses them, alas! These fugitive hours,
Chasing flitting passion and cheap sensuousness,
Thinking that God has not, of creative power,
But songs and large banquets, laughter, voluptuousness!

Time wasted in pleasure flies by before he knows.
Imprudent! Is he sure of tomorrow, today?
Wasting his time away, he ignores what he chose;
Someone other than him holds the count of his days.

Just as he leans over a small somber of thoughts
That in this marvelous feast, meeting his desires,
Drunk, he sees suddenly, from his forehead down brought,
Falling along flowers the hairs he admires.

When all his hatched-up plans come empty, tumbling down,
When all his illusions fade down the horizon,
When his ending of life causes nothing but frown,
Drying his well of days, his free flow of seasons,
That's when, all staggering, he yells out, demands,
And says, "Did I drink all the liquor that was there?"
No one else here to blame, no one to reprimand,
For draining together his soul and all his care.

But no one to reply, so sad and all haggard,
With his cold, feeble hands and battling exertion,
In vain he comes searching, stirring with great regards
The pile of lifeless ash, of the past, the notion.

II

So we're all heading there. But you, with strong spirit
And with heart full of love, you reply, "So be it
If time's always flying
And if a word always carries along its path,
Every which way it finds, everything on its raft;
Humans and days passing!"

For you are of that kind that alone can survive
Over Dante, Mozart, into all books can dive
With deeply focused stare.
For you cherish fondly all immortal matters.
Nothing time blemishes or with its wings scatters
Is ever in your care!

When it's your time to think, you feel the pressing urge;
A blazing harmony from your soul will emerge
      With its triumphant airs,
With a more subtle sound than the wind's gentle flow
That flutters and vibrates, as lyre's sweet echo,
      The hearts' fibers and hairs!

In this great century where everyone's astute,
Where the world does battle, caught in tempest dispute,
      Screaming out loud their fright,
You managed to sustain in the darkest perils
A serene poise designed to go through vales or hills,
      Help you through any fight!

Remain always this way! Center of our love
Around which all gyrates, blessing from up above,
      The attentive sister,
Spender of indulgence, sparer of reprimand,
Woman of pious heart, so serious for her man,
      Playful as child sitter!

For in order to keep your soul refinement
To store within the heart, harbor deep in your tent
      All thoughts of pure nature,
What can he really do, after God, on this earth,
To mind, as the best sight, bringing you blessed mirth,
      A father in aging stature?

Deep Inside

Nowadays, pity us, sweet and noble maiden!
Deep down inside his core, man's heart remains somber.
A snake lies in his pond in a nimble slumber,
And wretched unbelief always crawls in his den.

You, who have never shunned, never scoffed, never jeered
At the prongs that the soul can suffer in silence,
Living a serene life, attentive, with shy glance,
With a determined mind and a heart free of fear,

If you were to ask me, you muse, to me, a poet,
Where did I get these thoughts that unsettle my mind,
That I face in the dark, that I live in a bind,
Like a reed in the breeze, worried as one can get,

Why do I want to know where it is the winds swell,
Why am I so thoughtful and morose that the eve
Sneaks right into your dawn, awaken, still pensive,
And up before the birds, before the kids as well,

Why when the misty veil has finally risen,
As though in a palace of which I'd take a tour,
I go down in the vale and there I freely pour
My mind to the flowers while I closely listen?

I would answer to you that I carry a foe,
The doubt that constantly keeps me worried, somber,
This old deaf-mute specter pulling this sharp number
Of showing half a thing and the rest to shadow.

I would say that in me, I question everything,
Each small hesitation that lands upon my mind.
If I want to believe, I can't help, right behind,
That my mind goes to work and to me heartaches brings.

That is how you'll see me, mumbling away often,
And just like a beggar, famish, with mouth ajar,
Daydreaming while seated before this door they bar
As if I'm here waiting but no one comes open.

The doubt! Most famous word that, in fiery letters,
I see clearly written at the dawn, in lightning,
In the immense azure, mysterious, baffling,
Clear to eyes but meanwhile, turns souls into fretters!

It is a common woe to us from passion nests,
Whose mind does not attain your calm still and serene,
To us whose frail cradle, risking utter ruin,
Had to battle fiercely the revolution pest.

And the superstitions, those hideous vipers,
Swarm right before our eyes where all is done rotting.
We carry deep inside the remnants decaying
Of the true religion that throve in our elders.

That's the reason I go, sad and always thinking;
That's why deep in the night, I scope and I listen,
Alone and on the road, walking to no haven,
At the time travelers look suspect traveling.

Blest is he who can love and despite a blindfold
While looking for his faith, can find true love instead!
At least he has a lamp, waiting for sunlight shed.
Blest is he, for to love is half a faith to hold!

November

When autumn comes shorten every hour she spawns,
Gilding their every day, cooling their every dawn,
When November gathers the mist in the azure
That the forest shudders, raining down golden leaves,
O my muse, that's the time, with heart out on your sleeve,
That deep within my soul, your warmth you come secure.

The winter sneaking in with its seasonal tone,
Your golden sun fading, leaving you all alone,
Your dreams of the orient crashing down as you stare
At the street, come and go, so blasé a routine;
Windows, streets, fog, and lamps, all that you examine,
All that the rooftop smokes to your sight want to share.

Sultans and sultanas, in large flock, take their leave.
Pyramids and palm trees, galleys, executives,
The voracious tiger and the frugal camel,
Jinns of ferocious flight, sacred Hindu dancers,
Dromedary riders, truly skillful prancers,
And the tawny giraffe that its speed unravels!

Therefore, white elephants carrying tan ladies,
Cities of golden domes and crescent expertise,
Imams of Mahomet, magi, and the Bel priests,
All gone, faded away, no more Mohr minaret,
No flowery harem, no oriental parrot
That would come embellish Babel's Islamic mists!

It's winter in Paris! And your accord baffles
Odalisques and emirs, pashas; all such ruffles.
In such a huge city, the poor klephthas scuffle.
The Nile would lose its bank, and the Bengali rose
Shivers in these cold fields where all cicadas froze.
Under this gloomy sky, the peris would stifle.

Then missing your dwelling, my ingenuous muse,
Ashamed, you come to me, lonely and all confuse'.
Don't you have in your heart, full of juvenescence,
Something warm and lively, my friend? I am so bored.
Seeing through the window the rainfall I abhor
Makes me pine for the sun that gilds my residence!

Then you held up my hands in your transparent palms,
And in the confinement, far from the least of qualm,
From my precious recalls I give you the sweetest,
My childhood and its games of recurrent love themes
Along with the sermons that a young girl can meme,
Now married and all grown, among the wives the best.

And again I tell you how at the Feuillantines,
When it was time to sleep, still young, in early teens,
How wild and vivacious I would feel at the time.
That at times, in the yard, alone, the fallen dusk
Would find me all dreamy, peering at the moon tusk,
Like a flower blooming in the dark summertime.

I tell of my prowess, flying on this old swing,
Hanging to this old tree, screeching under the strings
To my mother causing eternal load of fright!
And I tell you the names of all my Spanish friends,
Madrid with its college, where boredom is a trend,
And for the emperor, the childish wars we fight!

About my dear father and about this young girl
Who died, she was fifteen, as young as a fresh pearl.
But you really enjoy the early love stories,
Butterfly young and fresh, with wings still soft and wet,
That grows strong and able, that one finger can pet,
Golden swarm that offers just one-day reveries.

The Shadow

He said to her, "Your songs are so sad! What's with you?
Concerned angel, why sob so much and all night through?
Tell me why, my sweet dove, loving and so docile,
Like a rush that the wind has bent with shoving style,
Lean your languishing head, at times overshadowed?
You have to be happy; springtime now is aglow.

April, the golden month, amid all its zephyrs,
The fragrance, the singing, the kiss, and the laughter
And all these lovely talks whispered softly in ears,
Love returns to the hearts just like the flowers here!

So she replied to him with a soft-spoken tone,
"My friend, you stand so strong, sure of God on his throne.
With eyes set on your goal, you go straight, confident,
No fear of the morrow, no yesterday torment,
And nothing comes trouble for your delighted soul,
The shade of pink that life hands you as steady dole.

"But I cry! So dreary, following your strong pace,
Suffering all these blows eluding your keen face,
Made of similar clay but lacking the strong hope.
I suffer in this world. You sing in other scope.

"All saddens me: the end that my poor mind, baffles,
Bitterness of the mind that comes, the heart, stifle,
The pungent jealousy of another woman
Ready to tear you up, coveting married men,
And destiny that shoves till for us rings the toll,
Alas! At every dusk, I sink more in my hole!

"You go forth, I follow. You step up, I tremble.
And while together we form a good ensemble,
But you seem to forget, walking, humble and strong,
All the many facets that to the world belong.
I drag my wounded self, hardly keeping your prance,
For without its spirit, a soul stands not a chance."

The Great All

If ever they told you the art of poesy
Is an eternal flow of trite delicacy,
That it's the noise, the crowd closely keeping your pace,
The idling fantasy in a golden saloon
Where the rhyme flies, toppled by some rhyme pleasant tune,
Oh! This thought please erase!

O you, sacred poets, disheveled and sublime,
Go and spread out your souls at every leisured time
Over the snowy peaks by the cold winds battered,
Over pious deserts where the spirit convenes,
Over forests that fall strips of their lovely scenes,
Over the dormant lakes by vales safely cloistered!

Wherever dear nature is gracious and lovely,
Where the grass springs thicker for herds to graze fondly,
Where the kid comes nibble the blooming laburnum,
Where sings the lone shepherd under some old arcade,
Where the soft evening breeze whips, with the clear cascade,
The rock now rendered numb.

Wherever the feather or the wool flake comes land,
Whether it's in the sea or some far meadowland,
A mighty old forest with unsteady foliage,
Isles with deserted soil, lakes of peaceful surface,
Mountains, oceans, snow, or sand, sea or living place,
Waves, furrows anywhere mighty winds come pillage.

Wherever the great dusk inflates the oak shadows,
Wherever, with the hills, the hills come and cross rows,
Wherever there are fields, harvests, any city,
Wherever juicy fruits hang down weary branches,
Wherever little birds drink dew from the trenches,
Shout your felicity!

Go in every forest, go in every valley.
Create a symphony from nature's dear follies!
Search in your surroundings, all spread out to your sight,
Be it in winter prongs or in summer frenzies,
The hidden sounds that spill for jolly ears to seize.
Take heed to the clamors of the Highest of Heights!

God moves in everything! The world is His temple.
His living work of art that He blesses ample.
All to Him give praises. To Him alone all go.
He created it all amid joy and laughter;
The star that shines above, the flowers mute blather,
Under His sole care grow!

Take it all within you. Take it all in, poets!
The green lawns and the brooks; take all that He besets:
The traveler at night whistling his fear away,
Those very first flowers that February, astound,
The waters, the pure air, the fields, and the dull sounds
From heavy chariots trolleying the forest way.

Brothers of the eagle! Treasure the wild mountain.
Mostly at these hours, the blowing winds sustain
A wind loud and heavy, with a strong crescendo,
To fill the air around with clouds spreading shadow
And push on the edges of the abyss below
The trees bearing their foe!

Contemplate the divine pureness of the morning,
When the brume flakes fill up the gullies in falling,
When the sun half hidden by the forest treetops,
Shining its blazing sphere, indented from afar,
Grows as the cupola, golden like in Qatar,
Of a palace of which the oriental style pops!

Come inhale the evening! This time, in the shadow,
Where the obscure landscape, with various shapes that grow,
Disappears, of somber trails of rivers' strange guise,
When the mount whose peak tops, far in the horizon,
Portrays a giant leaned, in this given motion,
On an elbow his size!

If you bear deep inside, living and well packed in,
An internal cascade of thoughts and dreamy scenes,
Of feelings and of love, of fiery passion,
To make it more fecund, very often go change
It, with your universe, too real to rearrange!
Blend your soul completely to God's great creation!

For, O holy poets, this art is so sublime!
Simple, divers, and deep, mysterious in each rhyme,
Fugitive, like water that none can come reroute,
Sung over as echo in every God's creature,
When under your fingers you hear exhale nature
In the loveliest shout!

Hope in God

Have faith, my lovely child! Tomorrow and again
And again long after! Believe in your future!
Hope at every sunrise; when dawn nature, regains.
Pray to your loving God; the whole world He nurtures.

Our foibles, dear child, have caused us all our pain.
Just maybe by begging, staying down on our knees,
After having repaid those His virtues sustain,
And then the true contrite, God will attend our needs!

Sunsets

I

I love the eventide with dusk serene and clear
That either paints in gold the manors around here,
Throning deep into the foliage,
That either far away, from the heat, spills its haze,
Or either the sunrays, human eyes to amaze,
Makes burst freely from each cloud cage.

Oh! But take a load there! See all those moving clouds
Packed up above us all, by the strong winds allowed
To take shapes and forms amusing.
From their fleet now and then shoots down the pale lightning,
As if in some sudden, some giant be throwing
His silver spear to the livings.

The sun, through cloud thickness, shining deep in the sky,
At times does, equally, the large domes glitter by,
As shine the roof of small cottage
Or battles with the fog over the horizon
Or falls to give the lawn a neat diapason,
Like a set for a fairy stage.

Then all of a sudden is formed a crocodile;
It seems to be moving in the sky for a while
With fangs slowly getting longer
Under its big belly much somber than its back,
A pack of moving clouds seem to give it no slack,
Making its stature look stronger.

Then a palace comes up and falls under wind gust.
It appears to be shoved or just fails to adjust,
So in ruins gets all dismantled.
It cannot stand the rush of the summer sky race.
Its tower tips over, losing slowly its grace,
Then finally gets all trampled.

Those clouds that favor lead, gold, copper, or iron,
Where thunder, tornado, lightning all carry on,
Stay dormant with somber murmurs,
For God hangs all of them deep in the heaven dome,
Like a warrior would hang in the beams of his home,
His set of resounding armors!

Then all ends for the sun, propelled straight on its course,
Like that old golden globe, now reddish, feels remorse
For having burned us the whole day,
Goes fall in the waters and sends up in the air,
From the steaming ocean up in the azure fair,
Its string of fumes in bright display.

Oh! Contemplate the sky! When the sun retires,
At all times, wherever, feel your love rise higher,
Ponder over the string of veils.
Sheer mystery resides deep within this beauty.
Throughout the seasons, savor on their flighty
Aspects in the sky, on their trails.

II

And brightness fades away. Under their glassy veil,
Every now, every then, a star comes up its trail.
The night, mutely easing, descends upon its throne.
Part of the sky's still brown, parts, to darkness succumb,
And silently pushing the crimson to its tomb,
Darkness comes give nature what daily it's so prone.

And from afar you see, lightning all its windows,
With its tall cathedral of towering shadow,
Its palaces' towers, as well as of prison,
With its towering bells, its fortified castle,
That in the somber sky seem to gently jostle,
The city with its domes carves the dark horizon.

Oh! Who will carry me upon some high tower
To see the whole city at this sublime hour!
That I perceive the sound of this town crawling now
Stifle down her vague voice, like that of a widow,
When in the day, laments, like the Seine in sorrow,
The running Seine annoyed by what bridges allow

So that I can enjoy, back and forth and fleeting,
The headlights of the cars, in the streets, conflicting,
And people crisscrossing, like in busy anthill,
And die from the chimneys, the hearth remaining smoke
And, gliding the facades of the houses they stroke,
Many lights come and go with magical appeal!

That the old city rests, around me all dormant,
That a smothered sigh spills, as would in a lament,
As though from tiredness, she would exhale a groan!
That alone and awake, over her lifeless streets,
After all the rumble of crowd, ocean, and beats,
I observe the giant snore softly between moans.

III

Further, let's go further! Under the dusk's last glare,
Where I'd see my shadow in the fields and the square.
And then the town is here! I can hear, I can see.
So that I can capture what's running on my mind,
Paris that I can barely find
Buzzes still loud her buoyancy.

I would go far away, go hide in some bushel
Away far from the fog towering all her bells,
This never-ending smog hanging around her peaks
That even the sole fly, buzzing in endless search,
In meek murmur come finally perch,
Covers all the city can wreak!

IV

Oh! Now flying amid the clouds,
Let me escape, let me escape!
Far from all that is still in shroud,
Enough daydreaming within drapes!
Let me fly into other sites;
Enough it is of somber nights,
Follow a glare, search for a note,
Enough of dream, enough of doubt.
That voice from down below that shouts
Maybe is much better to quote.

Come on! Some wings or bring some sails!
Come on! A vessel fully armed!
I want to see the stars in trails
And the Southern Cross blazing charm.
Maybe in other distant globe,
The truth we will certainly probe
Under universal degree.
And maybe to the meek poet
Will be given the fortune yet
To decipher the true decree!

V

Sometimes, under the shape of large fallacious clouds,
Far away, in the air, vapors running about,
Shuffled by the evening wind flow,
Behind the masking fog, deeper into the sky,
Appear the golden mass, standing proud, standing high,
Of cloud buildings, in steady row.

And to the eye startled, seeing this spectacle,
Over some far island in the air pinnacle,

In the ether, freely standing,
The eye seems to perceive, under the heaven's dome,
With staircases, bridges, high towers, real airdrome,
Some new Babel gently floating.

VI

Now the sun has rested in the clouds this evening;
Tomorrow will thunder, and the eve and the night
Then the dawn's subtle glow with its dew moistening,
Then the nights and the days; time gliding, pacing light!

All these days will fly by; they will go in bundle
Over the sea stillness, over the mountain crests,
Over the river flows. The trees they'll go fondle
Just like the many tombs of those dear to our chests.

And over the waters and the mountain facades,
Furrowed but not older, and the evergreen woods
Will remain fresh and strong; the rivers will parade,
Carrying fresh water from mounts to sea in brood.

But I, under the weight of time on my shoulders,
Go by and simmer down under this blazing sun,
And soon I will depart, feeling so much colder,
Leaving the world as is; a vast and radiant one!

The Antichrist

He will come when will spread the last shades of darkness,
When the Giver of days will close down His torrents,
When we'll see all the stars, from their forlorn brightness,
Fade like eyes in dying torment,
When the troubled abyss will growl in the shadow,
That the hades will count the rows
Of his soldiers, all ferocious,
That finally the load reaching the supreme Dome
Will, like an old chariot, weary from sullied foam,
Break its axle from this surplus.

He will come when mothers, deep within their entrails,
Of its appalling noise, will feel the dark tremors,
When no one will attend the sad and holy trail
Of the just' funeral clamors,
When nearing the waters, without shore neither bank,
The somber thundering will come matching the rank
Of the impending performer.

He will come when all pride, all hatred, and all crime
Of the great covenant would have infringed the vow,
When the people will see, fearing the end of time,
That this all-crumbling world, Heaven will disavow.
And the stars will come crash with large trails of fire,
And in the sky, just as in his antechambers,
A host slowly paces, awaiting his roomers
Quietly, back and forth, will traipse the Creator.

II

Amid all the nations, he will glow as a sign.
He will come to settle the ransom of captives,
For the Lord will send him solely to prune the vine
And the final harvest to sieve.
The world will not discern, all stunned, deeply troubled,
In other life, if he stumbled
As a ruler or as a slave.
And in their mourning wails as in their festal hymns,
Deep inside they'll wonder if the flare around him
Is lightning or is shooting waves.

At times he will borrow from the heavens his charm.
Like an angel, beset with beaming set of arms,
His whole body will glow with shiny reflection.
His eyes brightly smiling, to any doubt disarm,
Will beam like the first ray of spring in first motion.

At times hideous lover of the somber darkness,
Horrid beast with large wings and claws of toughest steel,
Pale and all shuddering before his own appeal,
From within the earth will undress,
At every step he'll take, the stench that hades fills.

Nature will be all ears to his marveling voice.
His breath will desolate many a big city.
He will dictate the clouds the path of his own choice,
With his chariots, taunt gravity.
He will master fire, will walk upon water,
And the arid sand thereafter,

His footsteps will cause to flower.
And all the stars will come and light up his halo;
The dead will feel shiver when he will say "Hello"
As though rising from his power!

Rivers leaving their banks, black larva erupting,
He won't have any friend; he will own everything.
He'll lord it on us all, spreading his mighty clout,
And the world, which will feel the weight of his stardom,
Will be his mere conquest but never his kingdom.
He will be a master whereas God never shouts.

He will seem, to the world panting under his yoke,
Bearing some other weight made of a different stroke.
He will never get old and will remain the same.
The flowers sent to him will suddenly wither.
Faithless and unloving, the world will ask whether
Or not to call him by his name.

His mere expectation will never spring from hope.
Submerged by desires, like drowning in the sea,
His knowledge will frankly go down the shallow slope
And beget pure astringency.
He will affront the sword hanging above his head,
Placid, with the coolest of stead,
And mute, like the coldest of corpse,
And his heart will be still just like virgin seashore
Where, in some somber duel from a dead-end accord,
Crime will come slaughter all remorse!

And at the end nearing, he will grab all the rest.
He will shut the beacon of the last lighthouse!
God who beset Jesus with crosses and unrest
Will shower all his goods on this infernal louse.
Lounging in his pleasures as lording on his preys,
His eyes will only show, during his wretched reign,
The deep shame well buried while fake joy he displays
And the pride that rises from the despair he feigns.

From the hades bringing to the mortal his note,
His hands just burying his lies deep in their hearts,
He'll mix in his chalice, for wise men to promote,
Venom with his perfume, honey to toxin darts.
And like a somber wall between heaven and men,
He will attempt to place an appalling discord.
His felonies performed, unforeseen, will remain;
The frightened atheist will shout, "This is my lord!"

III

Then when this messenger of this great mystery
Will have, from crime to crime, perform his every stroke,
That the Blessed Virtue, hope all salutary
That all the hearts no more evoke
That with the seal of crime and sign of misfortune
He will have branded all his goons,
That his herd stands in unity,
He will depart the earth as one leaves his abode,
And his reign among us will suddenly implode
From that time to eternity.

The First Sigh

Be happy, O my treasured friend.
Hail in peace your sweet life and enjoy your good days.
Upon the stream of time, in their mellowly trend,
Let the waters run down their way!

Go, now that fate still smiles at you.
Heaven will not allow, do not cradle this thought,
Any gruesome day to follow your dawn so new.
I pray that I am heard; my wish for you comes through.
Destiny for us two in my mind is all wrought!
One sad day, I may lose your hand;
Who knows, away from you, one day I may languish.
What, already my clouds rain their drops of anguish!
I have loved you. All has to end!

And now let it rain down all on me! Already,
To the sullen absence and for new desires,
A tender love's in jeopardy.
Deep in your heart, I'll expire
Amid airs of sad melodies.

Yes, I'll die; my lyre rings out her morose dirge.
So young, I'll lay me down, streaming my souvenirs,
With no fear since I saw, face-to-face, come and surge
Fleeting glory, now the tomb near.
Th' eternal Elysium veers to somber kingdoms;
Glory, just like the tomb, appears as two phantoms,
Vested of joy or donned with fear!

Be happy, O my lovely friend.
Enjoy your blessed days in peace.
In the same stream of time, still with mellowly trend,
Let the waters have their caprice.

The Cloud

That mighty cloud, O Lord, to everyone's the same.
Pretty soon you'll see it, thunder loud from above,
Glean from the fields of light, the tempest with the fame
Of making pure lightning of the sunrays we love.

Oh! That a swift angel would breathe a tonic blow
To keep it on its track, your lovely eyes to please!
If ever it glides down, this cloud, on us below,
Will turn to pure mist with its breeze.

See, to garnish the dusk, this morning it was formed.
The fertile mighty star, with its unknown splendors,
Changes in glowing strings, the show the mist performs:
The genius on its throne with crown of pretenders.

The tempest on its trail is followed by thunder.
And joy remains so scarce, but in the soul that pines,
Love, bright sun from heaven, can come put asunder
The clouds that life in us defines.

Alas! Your lovely cloud, all of us have the same.
Pretty soon you'll see it thunder loud from above,
From the great fields of light, glean tempests with known fame
To give off pure lightning from the sunrays of love!

The Shady Side of Dreams

My friends don't go too deep into your reveries.
Don't go turn upside down your dreaming sceneries.
When to your wandering eyes an ocean appears,
Remain upon the shore or swim but rather near,
For the thought can be deep! A slight downgrading slope
From within the real world glides into somber scope.
Downward spiral is steep, and when you start to sink,
It becomes much larger way before you can wink.
And just because you dwell on some dark enigma,
Of this daring venture, you come back with trauma.

The other day, it rained, for you know, this summer
Brought its load of cold winds and of rain much glummer
Than the usual bright May, with sunrays that elude
To take the April mask and raining spree, include.
I had raised up the blinds with shades of gothic themes.
And peering far away, to the trees, it all seemed
That the sun made its pearls upon the still-wet lawn
Of the droplets of rain and from the window spawn',
To my delighted mind, there, from the bright garden,
The sound of kids playing and loving birds gladden'.

Paris, abalones, house, rooftop, and the cottage
Everything, to my eyes, was floating on bright stage
Caused by this sun of May whose rays with charming glow,
All over the green lawn, lit up diamond rows!
I took a mental ride with these three harmonies,
Springtime, morning, childhood in my recall trophies.
The Seine, just like myself, let its ruby-red stream

Roll down nonchalantly its down slope, and the beams
Of sun would come and turn into some gentle steam
The river to warm haze and my thoughts, in daydreams.

Right then, with my clear mind, I could see around me
My old friends, not confused, in their epitome
When they come, the evening, serious and faithful troupe,
You with magic brushes, stroking sketches in group,
You fiercely uttering verses with blazing wings
And us all listening, together or watching.
They were all together; there, I'd see their faces,
Even the absent ones of whom we lost traces.
Then the departed ones came join right after them,
With the same pleasant look they wore as diadem.
When I took a good look, through the eyes of my mind,
And watched their family, around my hearth, reclined,
That's when I saw tremble their visages, slowly,
Become pale and then fade and, irregularly,
Together form a stream flowing into a lake,
Lose itself around me, and shape of large crowd, take.
Crowd with no name! Chaos! Voices, eyes, all unknown,
Those we had never seen, those we had never known.

All those living! Recalled, buzzing within the ears
More than any basswood or beehives in full gear,
Caravans camping stand in the smoky desert,
Sailors spread all over amid ocean concert,
And just like a strong bridge over cascading waves,
Throwing from here to there, those who adventure crave,
Just like the sole spider, between two mighty oaks,
Weaves its silvery strings that often, the air, soaks!

The two poles! The whole world! The ocean and the globe,
The Alps with snowy capes, Etna's crater to probe,
Altogether, winter, springtime, summer, and fall,
All the down vales leading from mounts to waterfalls,
Then turning into gulf, and seas, to countryside,
The capes that come rising into great mountain pride
And the large continents, misty, golden or green
By the vast oceans with waves not so serene,

Just like a scenery, in a dark chamber, set,
Gets reflected by its wavelike, flowy and yet
Its passersby, its fogs, floating up like a down,
All in my somber mind, all-alive and with frown!

So then looking closely, with mind alert and keen,
Grasping all sceneries and standpoints that convene,
That the wind's gentle blow and the flow of seasons
Would offer to my eyes in every horizon,
Suddenly I saw surge from deep within the sea,
Next to the big cities of the two worlds you see,
Other cities and mounts, strange and incredible,
Sepulchres in ruins of time unreachable,
Filled with heap of structures, towers, and pyramids,
Resting on the waters with peaks high and humid.

Some of them would spring up from under the cities
Where the living would still bustle like busy bees,
And from old centuries down to the nowadays,
I easily could count three Rome in their arrays.
And while they would raise up their uneasy voices,
The cities would resound together in noises

Of the people's murmurs or the army footsteps,
And those cities of old, all dead and with no pep,
No smoke from up their roofs, no rumor from their streets,
Would die down and become beehives devoid of treats.

I waited. Then I heard a noise. The dead races
Of these fallen cities came and set the places.
And I saw all them walk, just like the ones alive,
And right into the air, they all started to thrive.
Right then, towers and ducts, pyramids and columns,
I saw the whole makeup of Babylon's old slums,
Carthage and old Tyre, Thebes, and even Zion,
Up from where trickled down all the generations.

So then I took all in the earth, also Cybele,
The antique face offered and the new one as well,
The past and the present, the living and the dead,
The complete human race, no remorse weighing lead.
And they all freely spoke, with words warm and tender,
The coat of Orpheus, the tongue of Evander,
The runes of Irminsul, and the Egyptian sphinx,
The sound of the new world, as old as you could think.

But what I was seeing, I doubt that I'm able
To depict it; it was like a standing stable
Made of past centuries along with many sights,
All piled up, not having either left side or right.

And at every level, nations, people, races,
Thousands of hard workers, living all their traces,
Would hustle day and night, meeting one another,
Speaking in their own tongue, baffled by the other.

And I'd go up and down, searching to whom to tell
The load of my concerns in this world's new Babel.

The night, with this large crowd in this long wretched dream,
Was coming down heavy, just like the people stream.
And in some scattered spots, where the eyes could not trace,
The more people there were, the darker was the place.
Nothing now was certain; everywhere was so vague,
Everyone going by in this make-believe Hague
As if to point at me the humongous anthill
Would open from afar, vales that were not tranquil,
Just like a sudden wind troubling the calm waters,
Causes a spume or yet the rows of grain, scatters.
Soon around, to the dusk, the bright sky conceded,
The horizon faded, and the forms receded.

And the man with the thing, the being with the spirit,
Came floating to my face, gave me a shudder fit.
I was alone, and all was gone, and it was dark.
I can only perceive far away through the park,
Just like a vast ocean with waves somber and dense,
In the space and the time, their crowd large and immense!

Oh! This double ocean made of time and of space
Where the human frail skiff traipses with steady pace,
I wanted to probe it; I wanted to touch it,
See much closer its sand, tread upon it, and sit
And carry back to you some of its rare treasure
And reveal if it is suitable for pleasure.
My mind then took a dive in the dubious waves,
And in its somber depths, it swam, lost in its crave,
Always ineffable searching th'invisible.
Then startled suddenly, with cry loud, terrible,
Dazzled, panting, stupid, horrified, and pitied,
It jumped back, for right there it'd found eternity.

Perseverando
(Seventeenth Ode)

The eagle's the genius! Great bird of the tempest,
Which looks for highest peak of the mount the tallest,
Whose cry proudly reveals the dawning of the day
And never soils its claws in clay or in mire
And whose keen eyes can scope so it can admire
As it soars the glow of the sunrays.

Its nest is never made of moss; it's an aerie,
A rock fissure caused by some lightning fiery
Or some breach of summit, terrible sight to see,
Or some crumbling old den between two high mountains
That seems by winds battered, hanging and uncertain,
Tween a black hole and ecstasy!

It's not the humble worm or buzzing golden bees
Or the green dragonfly with wings of autumn trees
That yearn for its young ones, all-gaping of hunger;
Nope! It's the wandering bird, in the night lost, unsure.
It is the foul lizard; it's the snake it procures,
Hideous, to its spiky youngsters.

Royal nest! Somber den that from a wave of snow,
The rolling avalanche, along its fall, narrows!
The genius feeds its brood right there with all its love,
Turning toward the sun their eyes brightly aflame,
Under its wings of fire nurses their souls untamed
Till they can fly down from above!

So why are you surprised, my friend, if on your head,
The cloud chose to settle, thunderous, full of lead?
If some unclean reptile in your nest convulses?
These are your first disputes, and this is your first feast.
For you, other eaglets, it's more claws than it's fists.
Each meal stirs fighting impulses.

Shine now that it's the time! And if comes the thunder,
With a dazzling prism, put the murk asunder.
Allow your august thoughts to simply have their ways.
Come put your hand in mine, brother. Don't hesitate.
Poet, take up your lyre; eagle, embrace your fate.
Come, rising star, come fly away!

The mist upon you dawn will soon evaporate.
My friend, be known! Eaglet of sun born not too late.
Come on and claim your name by all your moving poems.
Come. This sought-for glory can be so deceiving.
It resembles a flag back from war, unfurling,
Proudly all thorn from stratagems.

See the feathery star; like royal meteor,
It snowballs from the sites it visits as it soars.
Just like a young giant that grows day after day,
Your fresh, blazing genius, far from the given trails,
Dragging along with him worlds of shining details,
Will go forward and grow always!

At the Olympio, Calumny

One day, that one dear friend who, by your torn heart, stands,
Pondered over my woes,
And as he was speaking, your smile of unique brand
Blended in his sorrow:

I

"So here you are, O you whose the riveted crowd
Admired the virtue,
Uprooted and withered, fallen bluntly and loud,
Like a cedar they slew!

"You're at the mercy of this ridiculing throng,
Envious and numerous,
You of majestic stance who outshined for so long
That bunch so malicious!

"Your branches have fallen, and your proud roots protrude
To the eyes of many.
Alas! You have nothing that the earth still secludes
Or divine harmonies!

"Young man, there was a time they would revere your mind,
Your booming point of view.
Your name was among those esteemed as you can find.
Alas! You lost purview.

"And now all wickedness come crash on your fair lawn,
Gnawing freely away.
And the crowd all around came peering, and they yawn
From lack of care your way!

"With loud deriding fits, they surveyed all your wounds
And jeered at your sorrow,
Just like they count their lots at the dens of the goons
After a raid of dough.

"Your chaste and modest fame, with useful quotations,
Has lost all her luster,
Beset from every part by a gruesome nation
Like a nightly cluster.

"They're lead by your beacon at any occasion.
Of your most famous name,
On the wide-open road, you're the sought ambition
For any lad and dame,

"Where darts of any kind, in the dark of the night,
Aim at, as they take turn
Some shooting at your heart, while others want your might,
And more for your love, burn!

"Your fine reputation of which we cry out,
As though it was a dream,
Just spreads and fades away when together they shout,
Like foliage's loud themes!

"Your soul that in those days they held in high esteem
As a beacon of light
Is now like a tavern where lay down all the dreams
As food for hungry sights,

"So they come and peep at some cheap-rated orgy
With vain and senseless spots
And loud noise of disputes and wasted energy,
Knocking pans, knocking pots!

"Your enemies took aim at your great destiny,
Tore it into pieces,
Of your famous glory, trampled by so many
In various instances!

"They disrobed of luster your fame with their bare hands,
All fed by their anger.
With the same purple coat they put you on a stand,
They praise you no longer!

"None came to your rescue. No one pays any mind
To your heavy burden.
They only speak of you as being in a bind
And they all say, "Well, then!"

"Alas! Just to hate you, everybody convenes.
They've all abandoned you.
And your friends, all puzzled, look at you as they've seen
A scene from Waterloo.

II

"Okay, for who fathoms your candid, blessed soul,
Nonetheless, you're better.
Your river has become as strong and just as bold
To hurdles that met her.

"All those who came to you during this dreadful time
Without a hint of fear
Come back saying they felt, in the flow of your rhyme,
An abyss drawing near!

"But maybe if they'd look into the sea so deep,
In the depths of your heart,
Would they have seen this pearl so rare and hard to keep
Where sweet charity starts!

"They stopped right at the fog of your tormented soul,
But I, judge and witness,
Know that if they had gone pass the heavenly toll,
They'd meet its blessedness!

"But after all, who cares if the world comes at you
With thundering speeches,
That your name flies around as always snowflakes do
When blown off tree branches!

"Besides, what do they know? We should just keep silent.
Who gave us right to judge?
We who remain so blind of what is relevant
Unless God we go nudge!

"Certainty will remain as foolish as we are,
Relying on our sight,
A pearl much hard to find unless we reach as far
As the spirit of Light!

"Just like water, she wets then runs her course swiftly,
And man can never hold,
To quench his burning thirst, the remnants, to quickly
Dip his lips or his soul!

"Just everything we see deceives and fascinates.
Is it day? Is it night?
Nothing certain. All fruit from a root emanates.
All root its fruit, can smite.

"That very same issue that causes your sorrow
Brings me felicity.
Everything in this world has a part of shadow
And one of clarity.

"The heavy, somber cloud, scaring the poor sailors,
In their boat all crouched up,
To the waterless ground and the parched-up tiller
Means a bag of wheat crop!

"To judge one's destiny, you'd have to come and dive
Deep into his abyss.
What rests in the mire may one day just arrive
To fly to heaven's bliss!

"This soul is now purging, ready to hatch and spawn,
Meanwhile waits patiently,
Today just mere larvae but tomorrow at dawn,
Butterfly so lively!

III

"However you're suffering, you on whom irony
Wastes all its proud assets,
And feel persecuted and, by crude calumny,
Wounded in dark secrets.

"You fled, bleeding and pale, and down in the shadow,
Through your wide-open flank,
Sadness entered your soul, like into a hallow
Well dripping at slow rank!

"You were, wounded lion, enthroned in solitude,
Weighing your destiny,
With the dusk descending on your same attitude
Of dawn's keen scrutiny!

"There, thoughtful, searching for a place for you to rest,
A shady, peaceful place,
Daydreaming many times, dusk to dawn, in your nest
Some uplifting palace,

"Attentive to the brooks, the bight glittering moss,
The ever-peaceful fields,
At the virginity of the grass no one crossed,
The blessings all this yields,

"At times contemplating from some deserted shore
The skiff tossed by the waves,
Drifting away, undocked, rendering the hearts sore
That sailors failed to stave.

"Observing the green front and the somber entrance
Of the shadowy den
And the tree nibbled in by sea breeze's persistence,
Contorts its arms in pain,

"And the immense ocean with the sail from winds, bent,
When the sun comes to set,
The breathing ocean, like a big chest that vents,
In and out, the air, lets,

"From the top of the mount with infinite rumors,
From the thick of the woods,
You go meddle your mind to the many clamors
Of delight or of brood,

"Who, holding in clear scope, everything encompassed,
From eagle to serpent,
That all comes loud and free, over the mind comes pass,
All nature can expand!

IV

"Console yourself, poet! Maybe one of these days,
Love will come back to you,
And the whole world in awe will see coming their way
Your brightness, rendered new.

"Every spot of dullness of your ravaged glory,
Lustered in the morning,
Will shine like a flagstone, reflecting your story,
After festive dancing.

"In vain, your enemies will have baffled the world
Trying to deride you,
And along their highways, spread all around in twirls
Your deepest secrets too.

"In vain, they'll shed on you their humiliated rage,
On your assaulted name,
Like a dog chews over, in a rabid carnage,
Some old flesh left untamed.

"They will never prevail in their mischievous plots,
All these circling vultures.
They will just fade away; like in the reeds get caught
The first shades of azure.

"They will always harbor in their hearts all the hate
That Satan spews to God,
But a Word will suffice to quickly suffocate
Their mouths of smoldering rods.

"And they will all vanish, and the crowd, in delight,
Will watch with tenderness,
Spring up from these rubbles, piled up by envious smite,
Your majestic kindness!

"Meanwhile, come and behold, have pity on this bunch
That ignores your lyre
And all over the place spreads around with no hunch,
Mislead to the mire.

"In this somber chaos, never blest by the dawn,
Let crawl the ignorant,
The pompous arrogant, bawling his angered yawn,
Like a muddy torrent.

"The lovely wretchedness with her deceiving stare,
Misleading in the core,
Woman with floating robe, who subtly comes ensnare
Fools like never before.

"The speakers who inflate their words with loud accents
When we listen to them
And this bunch of lawless, cultureless that goes rant
That a mere gale, can't stem.

"The bootlickers that bow with their familiar charm,
Crawling down, bending low,
And the conceited ones that, like in ivy farms,
Climb all over the flow!

"No, my friend, you are not bearer of the same crate
As those one-day suckers.
They are vile, and you're not. Their yoke is made of hate,
Yours of love's the trucker.

"You should never meddle with midgets all so mean
With the venom they pour,
For it must be uphold when you see sublime scenes
Performed by the dear Lord

"Far away from the vile trail that people follow,
After some illusion,
Plow hard your great spirit, digging deep the furrows,
Fueled up with your passion!"

And when he was all done, you who pure hatred drives,
You replied with a voice, for a tad, rendered tamed,
Voice that sounded like yours but in part not the same,
Like the mighty ocean when the river arrives,

"No need to console me. And yourself, don't afflict.
I am calm. I am cool.
I do not set my mind on this petty conflict.
I attend higher school.

"Human beings are better than you can think, my friend.
But fate is yet so cruel.
She gives gas made with lead or not. It all depends
To those she comes to fuel.

"But I dream! And I catch the giant cypress sigh
Round the ebony wood
And murmur the river and the bell ringing high
For the town not to brood,

"Recollecting the bird in its dull sudden flight,
The chariot pulling hay,
And the soft moan that purrs from the reeds, and the light
Shuffle when grasses sway,

"Listening to the waves, the ones that never sleeps,
The breeze in the azure,
I wander in the heights, up where everything weeps,
Every living creature!

"There I see, like a vase upon the altar set,
The smoking roof afar,
And at night I compare the lights heaven begets
To any smoky bar.

"There I set to the winds my dedicated mind,
Like the bird its feather.
There I think of the yoke of humans, and I find,
Sadly, their true tether.

"All moved, I contemplate all that I can perceive;
Ocean, land, and verdure
And afar I see man, magus with a missive
Straight from Mother Nature!

"Why complain, my dear friend? Man, at every moment,
Suffers numerous prongs.
I, in my somber night, have kept through my torment
That my pain still prolongs.

"From my bleak horizon, a bright ray through the night;
Love, the most precious flame,
Love that gilds deep in me what's most pure to my sight
And to my soul, the same!

"No doubt, in my springtime, unaware of so much,
Young, gullible, and stark,
I had my golden dreams, just like the living such
Who have dreams in the dark.

"I saw the flowers bloom in my life's early dawn,
Filled with loving-kindness.
Do you think I would dream, wishing that on my lawn
Love blooms in endlessness?

"The bubbles in my life that as a child I craved
Have all burst for long while,
And for my happiness, like castaway strength, saves,
I spare in downslope style.

"Who cares! I now go rest in this peaceful abode,
Pitying mostly females,
And I saw with my eyes fixed in heavenly mode
Where all the souls exhale.

"God bestows on each one his own share of burden,
To strong, weak, or coward,
Like a concerned master, with many task laden,
Divides them with regard.

"Let's be firm! The pure heart mirrors that of the Lord.
In trial or in success,
Let shower on our souls, lightning or sun galore,
So to mess or to bless.

"Let it rumble below this much-angered thunder
That from all parts besets.
Put on the shield of peace that will put asunder
Any nuisance we get.

"Go, no mortal can break with or without passion,
Though vainly obstinate,
This bitter law thus named by some Expiation
And by others just Fate.

"Alas! Whatever name that, crushed under their plight,
Human pride might give it,
Which it blesses or scolds, it reveals God's true might,
And man has to submit."

Fiat Voluntas

Poor lady! All her milk, in her head has submerged.
Thus in the cold saloons, the cheap talk had emerged
Among the lame gossip that carry the lazy
Yesterday, that she died; today, that she's crazy…
Alone in the graveyard, I pace upon the lawn,
The cold tomb where her life slipped, where her mind had gone.

Crazy! Dead! But then why? My God! For so little!
For a fragile infant, meager and so brittle,
For a newborn so soft, with such a rosy tint,
Who used to, at her breast, like fly to candied mint,
Hang, laugh, cry and despite her most fervent prayers,
Disrupting her sleep trend, wrapped in heavy layers,
Would keep so many talks, my poor delicate friend!
And who now is silent for he had a sad end.

When she caught eye of him, her son, this dreadful night,
For she called him "My son," this so fragile delight!
When she saw her dear child, him all cold and so pale,
"O Lord, please have pity" twas such a dreadful bale!
She did not shed a tear. The milk and the fever
Cause of her perturbed mind, her lips forced to quiver.
And ever since that day, all mute and with vague stare,
She would go aimlessly, aiming to just nowhere.
She would look, as it seemed as though she lost something,
Her sweet departed child, caught in some somber strings,
And at times she would lean her head as though to hear,
From underneath the ground, a lullaby quite clear.

A woman of the world who, one day, in the street,
Saw a crowd all around, hovering, curious meet,
Just by looking at her, guessed her deep misery.
The men, looking at her, all pale and all dreary,
And her cold stare always seeking some faint bother,
Would say, "Oh, poor deranged! "But she said, "Poor mother!"

But really poor mother! For a smothered short sigh
At times would choke her voice, which would murmur, "O my!"
At times, it'd look as if, deep in the ashes caught,
She would search for some light, when really there was naught,
For the sweet soul had flown, alas, from her dwelling
And with it suddenly took all her reasoning!

They had so much told her, murmuring to her ears,
That it's life, that all dies and vanishes from here,
And that for some children; O mothers, hear me well!
That God, who lands us all but never ever sells,
To lighten up the load on this dreary journey,
Gives us a short recess, a few days, if any!

They told her many times, but she could not listen.
Her fixed stare straight ahead, she would vision often
The child with arms open, cooing, calling her name.
She had made a small shrine with all his rattle games.
That is how he had died, in two months, no efforts,
For nothing can compete with this infantile fort
That after they depart they go with their mother.
As the child expires, so the mother smothers.

A house is not a home when in it there's no life.
A bed with no cradle, O Lord! What a cold knife!
Sweet looks of a mother without a cuddling child,
A tender, engorged breast with no lips moist and mild.

After a long period, heart bleeding, eyes weeping,
After all the pacing on the tomb, wandering,
It did not take that long, as per mourning cycle,
Just a few weeks, alas, for her heart to buckle!
The poor lady gave up in two months of deep sighs.
First she lost her reason; now she met her demise!

All it takes is one bird to come perch on a branch;
Right there, another bird, in haste, follows its hunch.
From both, there is always one that would take the lead.
As soon as he had spread his wings, not gaining speed,
He fell. The lovely child came crashing on the tomb.
She came, died right after. It hurt deep in her womb.
So they dug up the ground, and there, under the lawn,
They put the wounded doe right next to her dear fawn.

And I say, "O my Lord! Your law is so austere!
Lord, everywhere you put a mystery to fear,
In the man and in love, in the tree, in the bird,
Even in the cradle in such need of the curd,
Ambrosia or poison, honey or bitter gall,
Fit to feed the cuddling or the mother makes fall!"

The Retreat

As I was just closing these adamant pages,
On these thrones tumbling down, wasted by their savior,
The war just broke out; and dreaming heavier,
I saw pass in a glance its face and ravages.

And I saw shuddering a quidam in sorrow!
This all-sudden lightning splashed right before his eyes,
He shivered, all flurried, seeing hell in disguise,
O coward! Maybe tomorrow,

All thanks to our soldiers, brave although uncertain,
Upon this wretched stage, this most treacherous crest,
Like an eagle often dives on a mucky pest,
Some casual victory our fears will come flatten!

Despite your cowardice, we must battle. Come on!
Fight, you gangster! It's hard; you have to. God forces
You who from the first start murder you had endorse'.
Let's glory to oblivion!

What! Even if you crawl like a perverted pooch,
What! Even if you squirm or worm, begging pardon,
If you must kiss the feet of Cossacks of the don,
Another Austerlitz? Oh! No way, no Cartouche!

There is no escaping the strong grip of Caesar!
Go battle! Fake lion! Your mane, they'll come besiege.
This is the Rhine; this is the Elster, the Adige.
This is the pit next to the czar!

War, it's always the end. O people, here we are.
To hear you ring the toll, I go on my tower,
Menacing angelus at this early hour,
Ringing dusk for the kings and dawn for men afar!

Rights, progress we believe were forever tackled.
Freedom we requested, exhausting our voices,
Here you are! But throughout the many cloud poises
Resurge the famous pinnacles!

We can see reappear revolutions' summits.
Good old time of the past, march, come on! It's a must.
The angel with the spear of fire is now just
Behind you with his sword to push you down the pits.

Mufti's War Cry

At war, you warriors! Mahomet! Mahomet!
Dogs are biting the feet of the lion they met
Sleeping, now getting more daring.
Destroy, you believers of the divine prophet,
All those drunken soldiers, always having a fete,
Practicing one-to-one pairing!

Destroy all French people with their forsaken kings!
Spahis, timariots, come on and go striking
Through the ever-somber scrimmage,
Your sabers, your turbans, and the sound of your horn,
Your deep-cutting stirrups, large plates of gold adorned,
And your equestrian rampage.

Othman, Ortogrul's son, in us, come and abide!
Give us your strength and wit so we can be a tide,
Spreading your kingdom to the ends.
And so we'll reconquer, you city of blue dome,
Molle Setiniah, that through their lame idiom
The infidels now call Athens.

The Final Point

Excuse the casual bother
From my dragging, muffled dirge.
But sad words from a brother
That recurrently emerge
Should be dealt with much smoother.

Never is there any sense
For laughter to be at bay.
When purging for one's offense,
It is so futile to say
That prayer is not worth pence.

Should I mourn, or should I laugh
Is the choice offered to me?
Misleading would be the path
That adopts polygamy
As a scornful epitaph.

Rather focus on the how
To shout out your contentment
And still poker face somehow.
Just like at the interment
Of a foe you long avow'.

He who once tango' with love
And reclined at its table
Rightfully will always shove
The sound of any fable
If not sent from high above.

Look around and try gather
A makeshift for your pleasure
And your bliss, push much farther.
Never one should go measure
The wisdom of another.

Peacefully the horizon,
If peered at so intensely,
Will spit much-needed seasons,
Maybe not so hurriedly,
To rear all daughters and sons.

But all remains out of sight,
Like an over-used adage,
Your intelligence to slight.
And all alone on your stage,
Your rendition loses might.

And you're faced in your silence
With ideas that gone astray
From fear of your rude cadence
That chased all their drives away.
How baffling for your audience!

Only one chance is given
To the soul to be complete
And all its scores to even.
When on earth you fail to meet
You unite in God's heaven.

Shut the door right to my face,
Burn the book if you see fit.
Nothing will ever erase
The true north of my spirit
And off-track him on his chase.

Once quenched from this living stream,
One will shun a stagnant pond.
Once love held you in esteem,
None, neither brunette nor blond,
Will take her place in your dream.

My first verse, her brown eyes spew'
Tumbling down, chiseling my page,
Opening a realm brand-new
Where my world lies in bondage,
Praying my dream will come true.

In the Church Of…

It was a humble church with rather modest arch,
And right in it we walked,
Where for three hundred years so many souls had marched,
Come to God's mercy stalk.

It was the end of day, and all peaceful and sad
Was that church we walked in;
The altar all-empty, like a heart love once had,
Had no candlelight in.

The evening antiphons where Saint Paul, in the past,
Set all the fervent hymns
From the meek choir loft, deserted by its cast,
Was just silent and dim.

The earnest musician who on all lovingly
Spreads around his fervor
Was not there at his post, and the organ, lonely,
Stood lifeless and somber.

The hands no longer flew all over the keyboards,
Stirring the gracious notes,
That in a while ago, through blends of notes and chords,
Would the blessed hymns quote,

Making them ring out loud, with skillful finger twists,
In the hearts of them all,
From the pipes shining bright to come bounce in the midst
Of the assembly stall.

The majestic organ stood in utter silence
In the deserted nave;
Organ, the sole concert that in subtle cadence,
The way to heaven paves!

The only sound able, with the water dormant
And the blessed forests,
To murmur among us, of the vast firmament,
The treasures, the deepest!

And the church stood silent while you lay in slumber,
O quiescent nature!
Only flickering lamps, like remaining ember,
Shined in the enclosure.

One could only perceive a wandering whisper,
A word swiftly muttered,
Just like in a forest, dozing off from capers,
A bird's last note uttered.

Alas! One could palpate, at any dim moment,
Under the somber arch,
Something grand and sublime, of holy enchantment,
Away by twilight stashed!

She appears sad and calm at the end of the day,
That church we visited;
From the empty altar, like a loveless heart lay,
All light had desisted.

And you kneeled serenely, all trembling and dreary,
Sinking in your sorrow,
While we could hear the sound, as in somber query,
Of voices in echo.

II

Those voices going by would profoundly define,
"Gladness, gaiety, delights!
We have the golden cups, filled with the finest wine!
The others have their plights!

"Let's enjoy! Life is short. Nothing lasts forever.
Soon everything must end!
At any given time, the soul can just sever
From its decaying end!

"Let's get from everything what it offers as best.
The essence of the flame,
The wine from the sweet grape, the flower, the mere zest
Of the female, the same!

"Let's waste it all and use of this life dawning spring
Until our last days,
Of the day, the last glare, of all that beauty brings,
To what the years come slay!

"Let's go until the end of it all, enjoying,
Riding high in the sky.
All that must end someday has, among other things,
The most powerful high!

"In the wine I degust, what I delight the most
Is the very last drop.
The most rousing savor, for any given host,
In it usually pops!

"Why sample hastily in any given thrill,
Missing its true essence,
Not proving that a pearl, ignored by the world still,
Is there by any chance?

"What good is to just brush what we so acquire
And hold on so secure
And to live out of breath, like a youngster tires
From running the pasture?

"Enjoy to the fullest, from this all come to life!
Heed happiness's call!
Like a blazing cinder of bright sparkles so rife,
Give life our very all!

"Let's not do like this fool that boredom holds hostage,
Caught right in self-pity.
The very best of fruits are always best pottage
When you harbor gaiety!

"However, the most sad, like us, laughing it all,
Their souls, we often stale.
To melt these loving hearts, the rays have to come fall
From gold or from female.

"They fall down just like us in spite of foolish pride
And their vain bitterness.
The most humane of waves, when a pitfall they ride,
Tumble in foamy mess!

"Let's live then and wash down, drinking from dusk till dawn,
Everything to forget!
And thus so joyfully the feast tablecloth spawn,
Pure sadness to beget!

"The devoted shadow of the thrilling pleasure
Is the unswerving gloom.
Let us walk steadily toward the bright azure.
We'll stay clear of that doom!

"Who cares about the woes, the mourning, the despair
That our joys provoke,
That sadness always lurks, in the dark of its lair,
From all we may evoke.

"But we ignore it all! Away with all the pain
And the morose remorse!
Always in every wreath that on flowers, depends,
To roses we recourse!

"What matters in this world, all else is a bother,
Is whatever gladdens.
Whatever brings a song, a bright ray or fragrance
Into our selfish dens!

"It's not later but now. The patient ones are dead!
All pleasures on demand!
It's a strong, bursting breast, maybe by boredom fed,
That we kiss but that fends!

"It's the flashy orgy that everyone yearns for,
That paparazzi swarm,
Where we drink and stagger and then we drink some more,
Disregarding the harm!"

III

And while all these voices, inflated by ravings,
Soaring from the whole town,
Shouted, "Good health, gladness, joy, pride, and thrill seeking,
Prayer chased all your frown!"

IV

They were praying out loud while you mumbled your plea,
"O God, my creator,
You set me to face up adversities mostly,
Troubling me, O Master!

"Have pity, for the skiff in which I now stagger
Has no paddle, no sail!
And just like for children, set an angel-tagger,
Along each female trail!

"I know that our life span is nothing to you, Lord
Almighty, immortal.
You alone are truth, light, and way we can afford.
The rest lies in dark stall.

"This I know. But this stall where lie all our hearts,
There, I beg for guidance.
Will anyone answer? The secret, please impart,
Kindle my clairvoyance.

"No one comes. But at times, I can around me sense
The heft of sneaky plots.
And just like for children, why do you not dispense
Angels as female lot?

"O Lord, around my hearth, there's no happy family,
No one to call my own,
No majestic palace standing high, mightily,
No dew upon my lawn,

"Or the blessed beacon that helps you choose the way,
No pity, no goodness,
Alas! Not a mere friend to come brighten your day
Or a loving caress.

"O Lord, all around me, nothing remains standing.
I sadly vegetate,
Forsaken and disowned, there, in rubbles lying,
Just like what you negate!

"Yet I did nothing wrong to this great world of steel,
And this you know so well.
All my dealings are screened, standing with clean appeal,
Before your divine smell.

"I share with my brethren all that I do possess.
I call nothing my own.
But no one cares for me, while I, in all fairness,
All for them I disown!

"Never have I uttered, for the sake of your name,
Any word of protest!
To anyone I met, wondering the Way you name,
I taught them your conquest.

"You know it well. But, Lord, the tears that drench my face,
Who will come and wipe them?
All that I have I lose. All I owe is erased.
I have nothing to claim.

"I have no happiness. No fun was in my stall.
You set it up this way!
All the rays of my sky that I try to recall
Fade in thunder dismay.

"I no more have in me the never-ending flow
Of the day and the night.
My mind ever deepens at every tomorrow
Amid a gloomy plight.

"They say that you attend to the souls in turmoil.
You strong Spirit, impart.
Sustain my steps, O Lord, sustain me while I toil,
For my world's torn apart!"

V

And I was observing as she was praying God
Near the tabernacle;
She was sweet and solemn, pouring out her load;
Most tender spectacle.

So I told her, trying not to trouble her stance,
The poor girl all in tears,
If she would, in the dark, hear, just by any chance
A voice ring in her ears,

For all throughout the years, just like at any dawn,
Joy, ecstasy, sorrow,
An altar that can hear a woman her tears spawn,
To her always echoes.

VI

"O madam! Why do you drag along this sorrow,
So much rain on your lawn,
You dame with charming heart, serious as the morrow,
Sweet as the fairest dawn?

"Who cares if this here life, unfair in every sense
For men or for women,
Throws at you every punch, laughing at your expense,
Though faithful you remain?

"Soon your soul will depart maybe, away from here
Toward better seasons,
Taking you to that land, from the woes of this sphere
To better horizons!

"So then be like the bird, resting for an instant
On that branch much too weak,
Feeling it giving in, still performs its sweet chant,
Knowing its wings are quick."

Eclogue

We wandered, she and I, the mounts of Sicily.
She's stubborn and so proud but to me so lovely.
The heavens and our thoughts brightly joined together.
How in deserted sights, hearts can be so peaceful!
So many flowers bloom that mouths turn kissing tools
In shadows of one another!

And just like two lovebirds, on every branch flitting,
We got to an abyss, somber, wide opening.
She dared to get closer to this dark, deep crater.
And despite all the prongs that her sweet hands, upset,
We managed, hanging tight to all that we could get,
To see this gloomy pit meters.

At this very instant, a centennial giant,
Knocked down right into it by some loud thunder rant,
In vain was contorting, down where no ray dares shine.
Where horrible vultures with hungry beak of steel,
Attracted by the brawl of which the depth was filled,
To tear him, all efforts, combined.

Then she said, all concerned, "Please don't let us be seen!
Let's go into a cave, shelter our joy scenes!
You see this poor giant! Soon we'll suffer the same!
For the envious gods, cause of his swift demise,
Jealous of his stature, of his majestic size,
Our love may want to defame!"

The Others…and You

The others all around went to mind their living,
Their soul, their desire, their instinct and cravings;
With them everything goes at the speed that it comes,
The ignorant action and the mindless outcome.

They haphazardly trail the project or the dream;
Any issue they find, any flow, any stream.
They live in the present and all that it offers.
They slacked all through their past; now they are true loafers.

They exist, and that's all. Their minds hover and doubt.
They go, oblivious of any given route,
And they lose all notions gradually. Sheer boredom!
By gladness, yes, by no, the day when the next comes.

They live for the next day, flitting from thought to thought.
No moral decency their choices, has yet caught;
No deal of any kind their purview, polishes.
When they sit and ponder, caught deep in their wishes,

Nothing comes from behind, from their depleted well,
To affect the aura of the next ones that swell;
And for their tarnish heart, love ought to be painless,
The past ever rootless, the future flowerless.

But you who lovingly kindle my weary soul,
Who for the past twelve years, angel with woman sole,
Watching over my way or toiling every chore,
Took me under your wings or in your strong arms bore;

You who, sowing pure love in every utterance,
Open up to the mind, like a shiny monstrance,
The inner quiescence by the outer stillness,
The meekness of the soul by the body fitness,

The goodness by gladness, and by gods' warranty,
The supreme chastity into supreme beauty;
You, my beacon, my goal, my pole, and my magnet,
You, channel of blessings that the heavens beset

Since every soul carries all around their aura,
All in you is serene, beaming like pure karat.
You don't ever disrupt the blessed harmony;
You ring among us like heavenly symphony!

Nothing clashes in you. Everything flows with grace.
Your soul basks lovingly in your spirit's embrace.
Your world that so seldom sees you shed any tear
In this hushed life you live, silent in your own sphere,

Like a cool stream that flows amid a friendly moss,
Is a charming concert of grace the heavens toss;
Goodness, virtue, beauty, frank smile, fiery glare,
All in your sweet nature falls from God's steady care.

And when they look at you so perfect, it all seems
That a solemn, classic, and most natural hymn
Flows from all that you do, your milieu to enchant.
The others are noises; you are a lovely chant!

Mulieres

Women on the earth are placed
To idealize the great all;
The dark universe we face
Opens up at their mere call.

Love retains within its girth;
From sea to the firmament
As well as nature on earth
All these are its ornaments.

All that shines offers the soul
Its essence and lovely shade.
God with women sealed the whole;
For nature, flowers He made.

What good are all these sparkles,
Blue sapphires, with no sweet stare,
Diamonds, with no spectacles
Of ladies' enchanting glare?

And in every green bower,
Roses stand as precious grace;
They stand with charming power,
Basking in silent embrace.

Everything that can enchant
In women finds quality;
Stone alone will never grant
Glamour without their beauty,

It will be utterly spoiled,
Like my love chasing you down
Nothing but a feel that's soiled
By a wretched, silent frown.

Infancy

The child sang, his mother in bed all exhausted,
With agonal breathing, peering in death shadows
Whose somber clouds over her frail body, posted;
And I could hear her rales while the child tune echoed.

The child was five years old, standing near the window;
His laughter and his game made a charming background.
And the mother, right there, close to the small fellow
Who all day was singing, coughed the whole night around.

The mother peacefully went to sleep under slabs,
And the child lovingly resumed his favorite air…
Sorrow is a burden much too heavy to grab.
God will never rest it on shoulders unprepared.

The Last Judgment

Where am I? What power brings me back to the light?
What hand works such wonders of miraculous might,
Bringing my bones to life?
O terror! Lightning flash over my frightened head.
The sky is all-ablaze, and thunder blasts with stead.
The earth of fright is rife.

On his celestial throne of resplendent azure,
God, riding tempests with tumultuous allure,
Appears in the blue sky.
He stands and then extends on the world His scepter.
At the sound of His voice, arises the waters
To cover the earth, mountain high.

"Come to life, O mortal, at the sound of my voice!
Implode, O universe, back to your naughty voids,
From where you were once known!
Of all the elements, confound the great order,
Shroud the glow of moonlight, give the sky a broader
And deeper nightly tone.

"You evil ones, shudder! For now your wicked souls
Eternally in hell, will go pay all your tolls
For the crimes you raveled.
You just ones, now dismiss your sorrowful recalls.
Come to me, come lively, into my bosom fall.
Of my kindness revel."

Thus the Almighty spoke; the world simply awaits.
Only the trumpet blasts that Gabriel creates
Are heard in the heavens.
The meek comes and receives his promised benefits;
The godless, now reaping his rightful demerits,
Go burn at sin expense.

At this dreadful signal, the smoldering mountains
Spew all over the world what they so long contained
Of larvae red ablaze.
And suddenly the earth crumbles in an abyss;
Its famous monuments and palaces of bliss,
From their stands, are all grazed.

There, fire and water, the shadows and the light
In an ordered chaos, carrying the grim blight,
Smother the world heartbeats.
The horrible cipher of the earth takes conquest,
And putting down its scythe, the angel comes attest,
Of evil the certain defeat.

To You

Lyre, idling so long, awaken already!
It comes up, and our hymns will salute him always.
This day, her sweet name remedies
This most blessed of given days.

O virgin! From day 1, God revealed you to me,
Fine and pure; and dreaming over my puzzling fate,
Like a lovely bright star, amid misty armies,
From my pubescent years, I could see you radiate!

Right then I said to you, "O you, my shining hope,
Come to me. Share a bliss, one that will have no end."
For at that stage of life, ignoring the steep slope,
The past had not smeared yet my futuristic trend.

This tender care flourished into a burning flame.
I regretted that time, gone to never return,
Where my whole life stuck to your name
Was but a young child's dream, lulled by caring concerns.

Today, awakening its dream-stricken victim,
In lieu of the gladness that I had so dreamed of,
Somber, before my eyes, clouded by hopeful steam,
With a most wretched shriek, sadness swooped from above!

All alone in this life, Alas! Of reef scattered,
You have to drink the gall that offers the chalice.
Deprived of help in the matter,
What can an orphan make of this?

If the celebrated of a day, are adorned,
It fades, its clothes shredded and by ashes sullied
And to it, the day one was born
Is like the one he is buried!

It is within this world, with no life and somber.
Panting under this plight, living as in exile,
Only toward heaven, even in its slumber,
It begs for some solace with tears that won't defile.

But you, come chase my fears. Come and follow me, please.
Tear from deep within me this malevolent trait.
Come on and live my life, my troubled sea, appease.
I suffered long enough, Virgin, for a clean slate!

Oh! With your precious smile, my life, come embellish!
The dearest mirth still is within the realm of love.
Forever I'll uphold this light I so cherish.
Come, I am in the dark; you're the light I dreamed of.

I am really seeking some everlasting fame,
And if I have to reap such treasured dignity,
Don't worry! Your dear one won't let his famous name
Disturb his dear felicity.

Let's bask in subtle charms dribbling from the chaste bond.
That the glow of true mirth shields us from eyes for sure!
The snake crawling around the pond
Will never hear two birds flying in the azure!

If ever my young life, set to battle so much,
If my uncertain fate troubles your candid mind,
Then go away from me, my dear spouse, my first crush,
But as my mother, please be kind!

Real soon I'll fall asleep peacefully, unbothered,
Happy if in the night, spreading her dormancy,
A cold eye would offer, a string of sobs smothered,
To my forgotten lute, on my tomb vacancy!

You, remain untroubled by the blows your way, sent
And be that you never, while groaning in your turn,
Regret the one, who left, not whispering a plaint,
Who loved you so much that it burned!

On the Dune

Now that my time dwindles as if it were a torch,
That I have performed all my chores,
Now that I stand alone looking at my tomb porch
Through years of mourning that I bore

And that in this azure I pondered for so long,
I see fade, deep in the abyss,
Like a whiff of the past carried by whirlwind strong,
The string of my periods of bliss.

Now that I freely say, "One day, we are winners,
Then the next day all turn to lie!"
I am sad as I walk, poor skiffless mariner
Heavy laden with dreams that died.

And I look up to see beyond mounts and valleys,
Far behind the relentless waves,
Take flight, carried away by the winds in volley,
The cloud summits constantly shaved.

I hear the blowing wind, the sea crashing ashore,
The man gleaning the ripen sheaf,
And I face, deep inside, as I pondered before,
All that to me can cause some grief.

At times I lay myself, immobile and silent,
Right on the rare grass of the dune
Until the time of day, when sorrow to relent,
The glow much softer of the moon.

She glows with subtle rays, cajoling and dormant,
In the dark abyss of azure,
And despite the quiet and somber firmament,
We trade loneliness and torture.

What became of my days? Where have they all vanished?
Does anyone remember me?
Do I still have the glow that I so long cherished,
Glow of a time much less gloomy?

Has it all flown away? Alone, weary I beef;
I call but get back no reply.
O winds! O mighty sea! Am I but just a whiff?
That mighty winds to waves, apply?

Will I one day gather what I so long treasured?
Deep within me the evening falls.
O earth that blowing winds come slowly disfigure,
Am I the specter, you, my stall?

Have I wasted it all life, love, joy, even hope?
Patiently I ask and implore.
In my urns I topple; I feverishly scope
For some last drop as an encore.

But since the souvenir begets bitter remorse!
Since memories bring silent tears!
That I feel the shiver, precursor of the corpse,
Sowing in every human fear!

As I hear the winds blow bitterly, I ponder
On the flow of majestic waves;
The summer nature, gilds, the shore and I wonder,
At blue thistles the dune still saves.

From a Teen Poet

A somber and mournful sadness
Hovered upon our gloomy hearts,
But now shines aglow joyfulness.
The winning lilies topped the charts.
Long live the king, et cetera.

Go back, you dark demon of war,
To the hades where you were spewed.
Under such a debonair tsar,
No enemy will France include.
Long live the king, et cetera.

Now this perfidious marshal,
This Ney will soon meet his demise.
Tremble, cohort the world appalls.
Jacobins come and get chastised.
Long live the king, et cetera.

O you that a fleeting glory
Had dazzled for such a long-time,
Erase this error so sorry.
Cherish Louis; he is our prime.
Long live the king, et cetera.

And you that the rampaging sea
Threw up upon our virgin shore,
Tyrant, on us no more we'll see
Your rage comes down just like before.
Thanks to the king of whose presence
Chased away the vile ringleader,
Now we have peace and abundance.
My friends, let's all shout together,
"Long live the king and long live France!"

The Corsican now bit the dust;
Louis is loved by all Europe;
The eagle with murderous lust
With the lilies could never cope.
Long live the king whose mere presence
Brought us back treasured happiness.
He brings back to us abundance.
My friends, let's together witness,
"Long live the king and long live France!"

Dolorosae

Mother, it's been twelve years since our daughter is gone.
Ever since I, the dad, and you the woman, strong,
Have never spent one day, God knows it this I'm sure,
Not cherishing her name with prayer and love pure.

We adopted this grim and charming attitude
To welcome her shadow amid our solitude,
To feel her float around, to hear her shuffle by
While we'd be on our knees to softly pray and cry.

We remained devoted to this painful ritual,
Tenderly recalling this dear nest with factual
Thoughts of them now taken like you do two swallows.
Mother, we kept going, surfing our sorrow.

We did not lose patience one toward other
Or asked for a relief or even to smother
The pain with blocking out souvenirs of her name.
Yes, ever since that day, when nothing was the same,

The azure, the fields, the flowers, the star, the dawn,
And the many splendors that nature often spawns,
Toward the living three children that God saved us,
With the loving blessings that He still sends the Just,

We still have overcome various twists of this fate;
What they call rightly woes, adversities, and hate
With no flexing, trembling, or cursing the pitfalls,
Strengthening the sadness and the coffins, recall.

Sufferings that endure the soul, the family,
To all the departed, not our daughter only,
The ancestors taken to a better rainbow,
All tears and subtle smile to all other sorrow.

The Feuillantines

My two brothers and I, we were very young still.
And Mother would tell us, "Go play but do not kill
The flowers and do not go climb any ladder."

Abel was the firstborn, and I was the youngest.
We'd eat our given bread with such a hungry zest
That the ladies would laugh till they'd trick their bladder.

We'd go to the attic of the convent to play
And there, while frolicking, would see, out of reach, lay
On top of some wardrobe a very curious book.

We climbed up one bright day, the somber prize to reach,
And I don't really know how we managed this breach,
But I remember well the effort that it took.

Twas a Bible, old book all perfumed of incense.
We sat down, contented, up there and in silence.
With prints spread all over! Oh! Wow! What true ravings!

We opened up the book right over our three laps,
And from the first word read, our kid passion was trapped.
And forsaking the games, we fed our mind cravings.

We read every morning, the three of us enthralled,
Joseph, Ruth and old Booz and the Good Shepherd's call;
And still captivated, we'd read again at night.

Like children when they catch a bird up from the sky
Call one another, fast, giggling, and surprised by
The softness of its plumes under their candid sight.

Veni, Vidi, Vixi

I have lived long enough since in all my sorrow,
I go by with no one that could bring some solace,
Since I can hardly laugh to the children I face,
Since I no more delight in the flowers that grow,

Since in the spring, when God sets nature in gladness,
I observe with no joy to this splendid affair,
Since I am at that time when man no longer cares,
Alas! And feels inside his ravaging distress.

Since the hope so serene of my soul has long flown,
Since from within this house perfumed by every rose,
O daughter dear, I long for where you now repose,
Since my heart expired, since my drive is all gone.

I have not backed away from my duty on earth.
My furrow? Here it is. My sheaf? It's over there.
I have lived peacefully, always with a meek stare,
Standing but yet inclined toward mystery turf.

I have done all I could. I have served, and I watched.
And I often saw those who laughed over my woe.
It came, as a surprise that I was hated so,
Having suffered so much and produced such a batch.

In this earthly prison with no hope of escape,
Stoic, often bleeding, falling down on my knees,
Dreary and worn out, mocked and jeered by many,
I carried my shackle in this captive landscape.

But for now, my sight dims; my eyes slowly shutter.
I do not even turn when I hear my name called;
I am always surprised, annoyed, almost appalled,
Like rising early dawn when I had no shutter.

I do not even deign, in my bleak laziness,
To retort the envious whose comments always spite.
O Lord! Take me away, down to that endless night.
I just want to evade, leave this world of sadness.

Futile Envy

O woman, with loving thoughts
And bleeding heart,
You see the flower I brought
And birds depart.

Therefore, you envy the lawn
With sweet flowers;
You want my jealousy dawn
When birds hover.

And you say, superb beauty
To the dull face,
Seeing how the lawn's pretty,
To the vast pace,

"Their life has the best essence.
There all is nice,
For when the flower expands,
The bird shows vice!

"Next to you, O jolly wings,
Lovely lily,
What use does the genius bring,
Even beauty?

"Pure flower and flitting bird,
You win all treats!
Virgil cannot speak a word.
You're licorice!

"You fly high in the dark sky!
What sweet fragrance!"
And the tears gleam as you sigh
From your sweet glance.

Yes, admire the swallow
And the bindweeds.
Do not voice out your sorrow;
Death has its speed!

For we all go in the sphere
Of ether pure.
Woman will shine from up here;
Man is azure.

For the roses glow much less
Than the houris.
And bird flights cannot impress
Spirits' true bliss!

The Statue

When the Roman Empire hopelessly fell apart,
Since just like for Carthage, destruction is an art
That's to any city availed;
When having all destroyed of greatness and of might,
This world came tumbling down, shattered under the blight
Of crimes and vices uncurtailed;

When it all expired, empty, rich like Tyre
Loads of slaves rejoicing, for they could retire
From their masters' most wretched yoke,
Drunken of wine, of blood, and of gold, following
Cato, Tigellinus, the star by just nothing,
Giants by eunuch feeble stroke;

'Twas a dark spectacle, troubling to every sight.
And the pale cenobite, of this, trembled of fright,
In the fraternity cloisters;
And for three hundred years, one could always perceive,
Upon this condemned world, just treatment to receive,
The continual thunder blasters.

And then sheer Laziness, Lust, Envy, Orgy, Pride,
Avarice, and Anger, every human joyride,
Hovered from chests of jeering crowd,
And like strikes of lightning under the somber dome,
The swords of archangels tore down the wretched Rome,
Flashing fiercely from every cloud.

Juvenal who described this universal doom
Nowadays is statue, as reminder of gloom
Under the trampled old kingdom;
Not a tree grows around, no grass lawn and no reed,
And from its baleful eyes, one can gather this feed:
To have peered too long at Sodom.

First of May

Everywhere spells the verb to love. See every rose.
I am not alluding to the shedding of clothes.
First of May! Love bursts out and from gay or jealous,
Pulling sighs form forests, nests, flowers, all of us,

The tree on which I wrote, last autumn, a motto
Retells it all around as its own, just as though,
And the old gaping dens, mocked by the laughing jay,
Wink their thick bushy brows, sending silent hoorays.

The atmosphere exhales balmy and tender scents,
Declaring that it's spring in all that it presents.
The grass gleaming freshness sprouts to the firmament,
Expressing gratitude in every warm moment.

The countryside aglow displays loving kindness,
Producing essences spread in breezy softness,
Sending anew around all their fragrant kisses.
Every bunch as azures, carmines, purples, misses,

With scents that all around seem to say "I love you"
Over the gulch, the pond, the field, the furrow too,
Making spots in corners of every given shade,
Spreading sweet fragrances of its flower parade,

As if its expressed sighs and its tender missives,
Sent to May that transforms everything it retrieves,
And all its love notes sent from its brazen kindness
Left behind the soft touch of their every caress!

The birds in the forests, with muffled jolly sounds,
Sing joyously their airs to whatever surrounds;
Everything comes impart to the shades their secret.
Love sprouts from all over, as nature self-resets.

The north, the blazing south, in the dusk or the dawn,
The hedge in bloom as well as the ivy, the lawn,
The mountains, every field, the lakes, the gusty oaks
Repeat their love quatrains every time the breeze strokes.

My Verses

My verses would fly lively
Toward your lovely garden,
If my verses could only
Fly like birds, free of burden.

They would fly like sparkles do
Toward your hearth, fresh aglow,
If my verses mere ado,
Like a spirit could wings grow.

At your feet, faithful and true,
They would all rush day or night,
If my verses only grew
Wings as strong as love's true might.

Tomorrow

Early, at dawn, when light comes resurface the earth,
I will go, for you see, for me I know you'll wait.
I'll go through the forest, my ship to you, come berth.
I cannot stay away too long from my soul's bait.

I will come pondering over my inner thoughts,
Untroubled by a sound, undisturbed by a sight,
Alone, unknown and bent, hands by one other caught,
Sad and the day for me will appear like the night.

I will not give my mind to the dusk's somber shades
Or to the sails afar, gliding toward the town,
And when I'll get to you, as the day away fades,
On your tomb, my treasure, I will lay myself down.

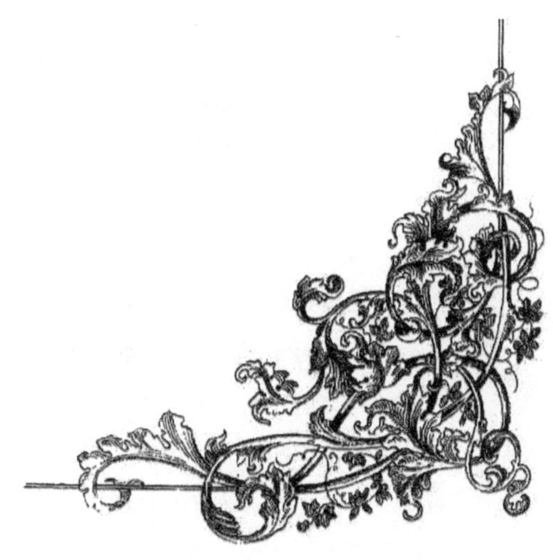

Charles Vacquerie

Never will it be said of this young man, O death!
That he would have opened the door of somber depth
Of this sojourn the world abhors,
That he would have himself, in this dreary abyss,
Of his promised future, so bright and full of bliss,
Spilled the cup of precious liquor

And that his pale mother, drowning in her sorrow,
Would so suffer seeing brought back this sudden blow,
In a shroud dark as its content,
This son, who while ago, bright as a dawning day,
Was lying wan and cold, source of wrenching dismay,
All crushed under death gnawing dents.

Never will it be said that he had died this way,
That from his loving heart, his life he would have laid
To save the life of my sweet dove,
That he would have freely followed her on that raft
Without the father's voice sending just a short draft
To his soul in heaven above!

In face of so much love, so much virtue revealed,
Never will I remain lost in somber appeal
Of words being so much laden!
That I would not have lit upon his tomb a torch
And I would not have spilled before this somber porch,
Stanzas, his great soul to gladden.

Not able to save her, he chose to follow her.
Be blessed, you so young, loaded with spring candor,
Of glorious hope for tomorrow,
Who could have stayed, living, enjoying your young age,
Having so much ahead to read up from your page
Of rising dawn with lovely glow.

To all that have in store the youth and the pleasures,
To the new love affairs, the lascivious leisure
By which all work is forsaken,
To the future, font of many flickering dawns,
To life, to the sunshine; rather chose to go pawn
Your life and be by death taken!

Oh! What a bitter joy for this charming young man
To manage to embrace, at this wretched lapse span,
His other half's most precious life!
That poor soul must have smiled, feeling in her anguish,
Through the sinister waves, at the time to perish,
That you came along on this path.

Their souls, in sweet cuddle, through the waves were saying,
"Why are you here?" She said. He answered, "You're dying.
I'm not letting you go alone!"
There, in sweetest embrace, meek couple in distress,
Slowly they sank toward the somber nothingness,
And the river forever moans.

Since you have been so kind, altruist, quick to douse
That you chose to perish, young man, devoted spouse,
May that your dawn forever shine!
May that you ever see the face of God shining,
That you're allowed to praise and in chorus joining
The cherubs with that child of mine!

Be blessed! That the breeze and the birds on the trees,
Flitting over your grave, come together to ease
Your rest in your somber dwelling,
The brook misses you blind, dripping in its sorrow,
That the budding bindweed sneaks in your tomb below
To caress you beyond telling!

To sacrifice oneself! With the angel exit,
Go behind the loved one, even into death pit,
Deny yourself of a future,
Give up all that you own, your dreams, even your blood!
The Lord with joyful tears blesses whoever trod
His way of love's selfless nature.

Nothing's like in this world, nothing under the sky
Touches these great heroes, brazenly living by
Love and the realm of its kingdom;
The genius with blank stare, with bursts of a winner,
He himself is baffled by the heart's demeanor.
The bird, the angel, can't fathom.

Sleep! O my lost beloved! Desperate lovebirds do sleep!
Sleep through the chaste marriage to the sepulchre leap!
Sleep to the sound of rolling waves.

Meanwhile, humans suffer, and the wind from afar
Chases the evil ones throughout fate insofar
As the sailors from tempests saves!

Or better yet, since death is not eternal rest,
Fly away together toward the azure's nest,
Deep in the sky's joyous abyss,
Where the departed just shines as a dawning sun,
Where the dead grim and cold is but lily that spawned,
Where the angel shivers in bliss!

Fly away, my sweet doves! Escape far together,
Far away from this gloom, far from evil's tether!
Fly through the ether with one thrust!
Fly far away from here, rude and gloomy winter,
To the gleaming azure and eternal center,
Calling all souls within its bust!

O my dear absent one, we'll no longer see you
Walking the grassy slopes of the hill born anew,
Sweet-talking through the breezy gusts!
During the month of songs, of nests, and of lilacs,
You will no longer sow laughter around the blocks,
No longer see the flowers burst!

We'll no longer see you treading the happy trails
Up and down just as if avoiding the long tales
Of the horizon vast and stern,
Searching somber retreats and deep bushy forest,
Where sunrays on the ground wink at whomever best
At a glimpse, their paths, can discern!

Villequier, Caudebec, along with these green vales,
Will no longer hear you laugh lively and exhale
On the breezy shores of the Seine.
Just like these charming sights, you're lying in boredom,
And the daring seagulls surfing the wavy foams
Won't dive in water much serene.

God who takes away life and gives back the ideal
Will to your candid souls, truest of love, reveal
Under the clear glow of his dome;
Taking you from this world, He freed you from all woes.
This all-loving Father traded flowers in row
To give you sky where all stars roam!

Go populate the flock of God's favorite elite.
Of this bitter chalice that you did not merit,
Alas! We'll finish the content.
While mourning your faces, drenching in our tears,
Basking in heaven's bliss, devoid of any fear,
Savor the joys of firmament!

Live on and love! Enjoy the infinite goodness.
Every single angel, glowing in blessedness,
Knows well, though under sacred veil,
The glorious ecstasy of celestial abode,
Of unending embrace between two souls that God
Turned into stars to His avail!

The Spring Maiden

There she was barefooted, lovingly disheveled,
Seated with feet dangling amid the green willows.
As I was passing by, I genuinely marveled
And said to her, "Come on, let's head for the Narrows."

She looked at me awhile; it felt like a whole year.
She sized me thoroughly with curious scrutiny.
I added then, "Will you? It looks so lovely here.
We could go through the fields, forge up our destiny."

She got up, wiped her feet right on the grassy shore,
And took another look from another angle;
She pondered. O beauty! With brain cells from the core!
Oh! How the birds were loud and joyously mingled!

How gently the river caressed the bushy bank!
Then she walked toward me through the large greenish reeds,
That graceful spring maiden, still uncertain but frank.
Her hair wildly bouncing, smiling, she took the lead.

Tears in the Night

I am the concerned soul unveiling his deep thoughts,
Robbing the quiet night of the essence it brought,
Well concealed deep within;
In this immense abyss where my query comes thrive,
Whatever my stanzas fall upon as they dive
Sounds like empty coffin.

And my mind infected by the darts of the doubt
Remains lost in the waves where reverie is stout,
With heavy, steady flow,
Awful lake where contorts horror, as pale mermaid,
Quenching with dead water, as a wretched first aid,
The rocks battling their woes.

The Doubt, lonely bastard of its grandma Wisdom,
Shouts, "What's the use?" Facing goodness in its wholesome,
Makes us forget it all,
Comes to us, bleak shelter, in all our endeavors,
Wondering, Are you there? Come! And we take harbor
In its manchineel stall.

The effect always sobs and then questions the cause.
Creation, in attempt to hear some, takes a pause.
Man to man is clueless.
Where does the soul begin? Where does the real life ends?
We relentlessly search for a hint in this trend
To ease our faithlessness.

We pant like a bird caught deep in the body snares;
Free and captive beings, the status quo ensnares
Every inch of our will.
Captives under the load of necessary chores,
We feel, of our throes, the web sneakily soar,
Our minds and souls come fill.

II

We remain in prison; the door cannot be breached.
But from a somber hand, unknown and out of reach,
Every so now and then,
Through the somber narrow, faithful souls, the true hope,
We perceive the rattling of the keys to elope,
Still caught up in this den.

But man remains submerged in the world that he sees.
A subtle alliance endless in frequency
Of the night and the day;
Is this world an Eden fallen in Gehenna?
We carry deep within the traits of hyenas,
As well as ovine prey.

Creation's sole display is a dimmed, unclear sight.
The eternal Being spreads both side of his might,
Good, evil, ice, and fire;
Human feels at same time, candid soul, somber flesh,
The bites of many worms, caught under six-foot mesh,
And his soul climbs higher.

On any given day, the soul's like a widow.
We witness the wailing of men in their sorrow.
We doubt, and we tremble,
While the dawn comes brighten the first yawns of the day
And while May buds flower every step of our way,
Magical ensemble.

But then what of the light, the dawn, and all the stars,
Flowers shining and blue, with diamond doors ajar,
Deep in the firmament,
Month of May's treasured breeze and children's candid charm,
If all is but fleeting, awaiting the alarm
To fade in a moment?

III

Daily fate wears us down, sad turning grinding wheel.
The vain human worries, sojourns although he feels,
Then dies thinking he walks.
We possess the second but yearn for the whole year,
And the true dimension that our destiny steers
Is close to dust of chalk.

The abyss where the suns appear like tiny flies
Contains us, where we hear only loud wailing sighs
Or plain scoffing laughter;
Toward the higher aim, there, in the great azure,
We send projects, wishes, and the hopes we ensure,
All straight from our ticker.

Poor dust, we sure would like to last, live forever!
Where is this tiny ant with name Alexander?
Where is the worm Caesar?
Each minute that befalls takes from us its own bite.
And we go, somber swarm, holding to nothing tight,
Like a bleak shooting star.

Like a battling army, we try to assail time.
Over the confused horde lost in the smoky slime
Of days that came and went,
Eternity still shines, humongous and stagnant,
And the dial, protector of time and its warrant,
Bedazzles and still vents!

IV

The minute that we say, "Let's live!" all falls apart.
The sobs all suddenly come along and take part,
Crushing all the laughter!
Your sons are dead; my father too, and their mother is dead.
O death! Who then goes there, dragged with such somber tread?
Who's this coffin owner?

They're taking it away to the shadows, to earth;
They're heading for the calm, the darkness, the cold turf,
To the brume with no end,
To the cold mystery, contorting in its veils,
To the unknown serpent that on any star sails
To kiss the dead at hand.

V

They take him to the worms, to naught, the Great Maybe!
For most of them never saw the light, the to-be,
Skeptic and too narrow?
The dreary negation and the hostile matter,
Flags of self-deception, their candid soul, batter,
Landing them but sorrow.

For them, Heaven's a lie, but man lives in a dream.
And they, from front to back, scanned of the book all themes
They have yet to fathom.
They live nodding all lost, steadily and meanwhile
In the void, somber skeins that the doubt firmly piles
Fall down in their bosom.

For them, the soul just drowns when the matter succumbs.
Their dream has empty stare and peers into the tomb;
Nothing is what they reap.
And everyone laughing straight at the starry dome
Carries deep in his heart, instead of hope of chrome,
The head of a dead sheep.

Deaf to the forest sounds, the somber organ note,
Everyone is a camp cold, arid that denotes
Dusty pieces of rag,
A bare cemetery where the quivering poets
See all ironies plane, along with owls that set
Shadows where crows come brag.

When the star and the reed tell them, "Hey you, have faith,"
They say to the green rush, to the star on its slate,
"You don't make any sense!"
When the tree, in their ears, murmurs, "He does exist,"
Those fools reply, "No way!" And if the oak insists,
They say, "Enough nonsense!"

Misery! The sower denied by the grain seed!
The universe to them should cater to their greed
With no limitation;
When their souls come joggle the vast infinity,
Gather not the being. They miss the Almighty
When rattling creation!

VI

The hearse enters the gate of the cemetery.
Nature greets the morning with golden reverie,
Smiling softly on this mourning.
Mystery is in all, from where the soul comes spawn
To nudge infinity; the star drags in the dawn,
And the man, his coffin.

You see the inner pit as a dreary manger.
There, stones scattered around, to the ground no stranger,
Sadly salute the knell;
They seem like cold eyelids open for the welcome,
And the butterfly says, "Why these stones so gruesome?"
The flower, "I can't tell!"

VII

By any chance, are those stones, for something, punished,
Mighty God, to suffer agony so hellish?
Ah! What we can suffer
Is nothing compared to trees battling cold breezes.
Under this appalling form, is it Cambyses
Or the Nero's affair?

After having enslaved their flock tight in their claws
And crucified humans to the wretched gallows,
Turn the world into shreds,
Sullied the soul and changed, under great disasters,
The world in pure mass grave and sent to stars faster,
The reek that the tombs thread,

After having passed through, happy in victory,
And in pride spread around all throughout history
Their claws mischievous
And monsters that foresee all human lethargies,
After having on earth being living effigies
Of evil treacherous,

After having filled up every jail and prison
And poured out so much crime to make the sea crimson,
All slaughtered by the sword,
So much somber carnage and horror unnoticed,
That the sun, in the night, would waver, seeing this
Bloodbath it couldn't afford.

After having gnawed at the flock that God pastors,
Turned over and over, as pure torture mentors
The atrocious capstan
Reigned under the purple or under laticlave,
Bent for thousands of years, Adam, the premier slave,
Under the vile Satan,

Is the hunter Nimrod? Is it Sforce's mantra?
Is it Messalina? Is it Cleopatra,
Caligula, Macrin,
And the Achabs through whom were reborn the Sodoms
And Phalaris, tyrant performing the gruesome
Those ancient widespread sins?

Is it Charles the Ninth, Louis the Eleventh, Constantine,
Vitellius, the mire, Busiris, man of tin,
The devouring Cyrus,
The Aegisthus fingered out by the cold Electra,
Would then be in that night, from men into spectra,
To tyrants' stones and plus?

Were these stones embedded, permeating vile crimes,
Stifling in the horror, sealed and devoid of time,
Envious of the bones,
With no air, no movement, no day, no eyes, no mouth,
Between the somber grass and crate eternal sloth,
Living in hellish tone?

Would they be, one may ask, a cluster of damned souls,
Condemned for thousand years with nothing to unfold
But a pile of remorse,
In lieu of admiring the beauty of sun glare,
With show of golden rays, would pitifully stare
At worms having their course?

Man and rock coexist down in this somber life!
Dream while still petrified in one's own horror strife!
Dream of eternity!
Devour one's furies roared out confusedly!
Caught in crimes and orgies performed so hurriedly
In immobility!

Punishment! Dark problem! Questions much too dreary!
What! This rock would then say, "I caused Thebes worries.
I saw Suze on her knees!
I was Belus at Tyre! I was Scylla at Rome!"
Dreaded captivity of lost cities' old gnomes!
O stones, are you many?

What has this gaping block done in this diseased pit?
Cold, dampened, and profound lugubrious hell fit,
Old chastised cavity,
Blind even to the fire that the night set ablaze,
He thinks and remembers…It's Tiberius! Amazed.
O my Lord, have pity!

This hard flint in the earth, drown, rough, and so uncouth,
Overshadowed; meanwhile, the sky comes in to soothe
The soul that just returned,
Envying the ass passing and dog barking frenzy,
Shouts clearly, "I am here! Living God, have mercy!
It's Borgia. Please don't shun!"

O good God, show mercy to all these wretched men!
Save these forsaken souls, love these accursed humans!
Open up these jail gates.
For the innocent's sake, God forgive all these crimes.
Father, please close down hell. Judge them at Your own time.
Pity the hangmen's fate!

From everywhere you hear cry out loud "Have mercy!"
The peoples naked, bound, scourged with accuracy,
Pitiful slaving bunch,
Seeing their master submerged by chastisement sublime,
Pity the poor despot and bleeding from his crimes,
Cry his pain with no hunch.

And the pallid nations look deep in the abyss,
And all these supplicants, for such tyrant as this,
You dear God, they implore
The slave upon the cross, the oppressed on the rack
Pity this satrap there, in the abyss, the pack
Says, "Spare the nails! Encore."

Serene God, look upon, with salutary glance,
All these forlorn recluse that the earth has in trance
Under these dreary locks,
Those convict whose prison is the inside of stones,
And raise up, by the just who for them all atone,
Those whom your mercy block.

Father, have pity of the monster and the stone.
For all these condemned souls, let your pardon be honed!
Formerly kings of wars,
These bandits on the earth wreaked havoc and had feasts;
Having risen higher in horror than the beast,
They're all sullen of tar.

Pity for them! Mercy, clemency, and pardon,
Refuge for the dear prince, as well as the worm son!
The wicked lost his mind.
God, let in the damned one! God, raise the infamous!
Give them back the blue sky, the tiger, animus,
Let the stone its wings find!

Mystery that baffles any mind pondering!
Ladder of the sorrow and of the rejoicing!
Night nearing the sweet dawn!
Smile spread with all its charm over bitter torture!
Vision of somber tomb! Are you of real nature
Or just other lie spawned?

VIII

The pit, just like flank wound of the earth, lay gaping,
And wide-opened, provokes the green grass shivering
And the shrub to wither;
She is there, cold and calm, narrowed and just lifeless,
And the soul watches rise, like a sign of distress,
Infinity's tether.

And the birds in the air, hovering in the heights,
Scanning the world around, comparing other sights
In the chores they contest,
Next to Vesuvius and the ocean compass,
Conclude when comparing this pit there in the grass:
This one is the deepest.

IX

Now that the soul has flown, nature comes claim her due.
Life chose; that was enough. This creature is now through.
Hey, dead, how does life spell?
He is now out of time, out of space, out of count.
They wheel him down the pit like a bucket you mount,
Is wheeled down in a well.

What do you want to draw from up these mighty fonts?
Why do you want to probe the improbable fount?
What do you want to find?
Is it the warm farewell of the ones we now miss?
Alas! Is it a glance? Or maybe a last kiss,
An embrace warm and kind?

What do you want to draw, humans, frivolous swarm?
Is this a shivering of this void left still warm,
A sound or a pale shade,
A letter from the Word only God can master?
Is it to put a touch of brightness and luster
To your eternity that fades?

This pit where the larvae opens up its dim eye,
In this appalling tank, this cistern of strong dye,
True abyss of sorrow,
In this obscure crater where you abide deaden,
What do you want to draw, you of minute laden,
Race of bleak tomorrow?

Is it the dark secret or the cold single drop
That drips from the stale dome as a specter teardrop,
Where nothing shines or looms?
Is it some subtle glow, all flurried and haggard?
Is it the scream of fright from those who dared regard
Behind the frigid tomb?

But you won't draw a thing! The dead fall, and the pit
Receives them with their soul with or without merit,
With name, with step and noise.
One day when the heavens will deign breathe life anew,
Only God will revive these tombs of me and you
From our eternal poise.

X

The earth, agitating the bramble on her face,
Says, "The human has died. Well, why bring me his trace?
Why send him back to me?"
Earth, make flowers of him! Lilies that soothes the dew!
From this mouth agape with teeth make roses anew
Natural alchemy!

Let this blood run throughout the streams of running brooks
Quench all your bovine guests; they will never get spooked.
Disperse these shreds of flesh;
Transform these mottled breasts into lovely violets.
From these eyes untroubled by sunrise or sunset,
Butterfly wings, refresh.

Give a joyful outcome to these bodies absorbed.
Bring out the great torrent that roars and then adsorbs
Green grass for every lawn!
Turn them to rocks, rushes, fruits, and all shades of vine,
In breezes and perfumes, great trees that intertwine
And furrows where grains spawn!

Turn them into green shrubs, into beautiful grass!
And that deep in your girth from where sprout any mass
Throughout their peaceful sleep,
The horrifying dead, breathless, with no holler
Feel shiver all over when all these corollas
Tremble when sunrays nip!

XI

The ground, on the casket where the pale corpse perceives,
Falls and the nest twitters, and there, his ears receive
The whistling of farmers.
And his sons and his friends brought in by sheer remorse
Do not wait till the pit is filled up. They recourse
And say, "It got warmer!"

The gravedigger, defrayed for his hushed-up labor,
Throws over the casket, the ground with dim ardor.
You who, warm in your shroud,
Dreamed of the endless time, this all-spotless white dove,
With this man now treading, your tomb, up and above,
O dead, where is your crowd?

Now begins the forlorn and dour solitude!
Never will you change bed. No change of attitude;
The solemn time pacing
Will never ring for you. Darkness makes you dreary;
The immobile wrapping renders you so scary,
With eternal creasing.

And then the gravedigger goes on to drain the pit.
He just saw some dentures that from the ground exit.
He laughs; he eats and bites.
Intones in a murmur some old and stupid songs,
A drink in hand clanging to whatever belongs
To what death so excites.

Evening falls, rolling down loads of inquietude;
The grass quivers and hums from hidden multitude.
The river shines aglow,
And the somber landscape steals the marble luster.
These hydras that by day are seen as tree cluster
Contort as the winds blow.

So left alone, the dead feels all gnawed by the night.
When the dawn comes brighten the azure with its light,
The sunrays are lovely.
The birds and all the love and the numerous tunes
Go to gild the cradles; but at night, free of moon,
All tombs darkness, rally.

He hears loud sighs around in the neighboring pits;
He perceives the tickles of the roots as they fit
The casket position.
He is all defeated by dear Mother Nature;
He feels a dark finger changing his eye structure,
Weirdest of sensation.

He feels cold, for the night, the mixture of his breath,
Darkness, horror, and moth reveal the specter heft,
Lying on the pallets.
And the corpse wrapped around by the many white strips
Shudders, and the four boards of the casket come sip
Sweet nothings that upset.

One says, "I used to close your safe." And the other
Say, "I was the strong door where we lived together."
The third says, "In good days,
The table where laughter and good wine came mingle,
That was I. The last one says, "I was night table
Of your love bed to play."

Come on, people! Laugh, sing; come on, the day's ablaze.
Leave all you have behind, leave all the joys that phase
With no brume, no conflict,
Leave behind the fanfare and the ball in its swing.
All these dead that he tucked as though they were his things,
The gravedigger convicts.

XII

They will come all.

XIII

Enough! And now leave the table.
Each one takes, in his turn, the train that's reachable.
Shivering, each one leaves.
Sing, laugh, and be happy and be famous as well;
Each one will, soon enough, fall in the darkness well
And his specter retrieve.

The crowd admires you; the sky brightens your day.
You are rich and mighty, popular in your ways,
Glorious and so proud;
Your somber lictors walk with ax preceding you.
And one day, near or far, all of this will be through;
You'll meet with your own shroud.

Alas! Lovely young girls, as sure as comes the dawn,
You dance still in the ball or you bronze on the lawn,
Treasuring your figure.
In any clear mirror, you can see candle grow,
But death on your foreheads imprints a virgin glow
Of infinite allure.

The conqueror facing the rising of his sun
Leans to see smoke away his sword in tail that spun;
Hand in hand, the lovers
Go by. The cradle sounds with airs from the tomb, straight.
The newborn turns into grim larvae, and his fate
Rattles as death hovers.

What they spoke of last night, they no more remember.
The wishes and the lies, the family members,
O dreadful nothingness!
None remains; it's all gone, forgotten in the flow
Of the things God promotes in celestial furrows,
So fast to man's distress!

O promises and hopes! Lost in the span of space.
Whoever promises, has himself, fleeting pace.
Fool who believes in him!
Promises all follow the path of blowing wind,
The path of running brooks, where dead leaves get all pinned
And all sights lose esteem.

Think about the true size of the void we evolve.
When you'll be in the ground that will slowly dissolve
Every inch of your bones,
Your folks wasting away their days that God bestow
Will remain in the light or their weakness, will stow
All to your mind unknown!

What you plan tumbles down, along with what you do.
See these great palaces, this feverish ado
Not proceeded in scope;
See all these guns blazing unlike ever before,
These horses running fierce up and down our shores,
Like loaded of pure dope,

All this will soon be gone, just like a singing voice;
Pyramid, you lord it over the tent's meek poise
Under the blazing sun;
You see it quivering in the wind like a veil.
Cheops, you feel, she is made of cloth and so frail,
While you of granite spun.

And you tent, you reply, "Long live the pyramid!"
But one day, running wild, like Nubian horse stampede,
The Libyan hurricane
Will blow his sandy might over all the frail tents,
And Cheops will sustain whatever Allah sent,
Simply saying, "Poor mane!"

You also will perish although you're wall enclosed
And no longer will be, O city that God chose
But pure rubble of smoke,
And those who favored you, those who loved you so much,
Will strike their hairy breasts when they'll see you in such
Degraded twist of stroke.

They will say, "O sadness! O turmoil! Civil war!
What city can compare to this city so far?
Her towers were so proud.
She was the joy for all through all her prostitutes.
She was the true beacon for the world destitute,
With her large streets and crowd.

"City! Where are all those who mentor your greatness?
All your lion tamers with lyre skillfulness,
Your relentless fighters?
City, have you been robbed while you frolicked at night?
Where then is Babylon? Alas! She lost her might!
All her might and laughter!"

No longer can you hear in you the grind of mill.
Not a single hammer hits a nail. And you're still
Forgotten by your clowns.
No one will come walking up or down your proud ramps;
No longer will they see the glowing of your lamps
That lightened once your frowns.

Shine bright to disappear and ascend to descend.
The grain of sand reveals to the ash that pretends:
Learn to swim the mire.
"Therefore, where is Thebes?" says Babylon, pensive.
Thebes wondered about Nineveh, in her sleeves,
Nineveh, "where's Tyre?"

Speaking at great extent of all he encounters,
Man wags the world over though closely monitored;
God weighs every action.
Every day that aglow brings its load of mourning;
Woe to whosoever goes mischief performing
Thinking there's no sanction!

We succumb at the end, after a senseless trip
Or making our first step; man from what he may sip,
The mother on her nest,
The king and his scepter, the one waving the flute,
They all go; nothing lasts; the good father, the brute,
The elder, the finest.

The races reach the shore that this old world reveals.
When the old fades away, the new one comes refill
With the same enterprise.
In the eternal pit where its fill, the tomb pours,
Man continually flows, somber river that roars
In dark seas of demise.

Every staircase covered of splendor or of gloom
Descends straight to the grave and through every door looms
One's very last moment.
Your sepulchre fills up the palace you reside;
Any roof on our heads, with beams from side to side,
Can fall any instant.

Stay awake, vigilant! Remember the deceased.
Be humble and mindful; of calumny desist.
Worship down on your knees;
Death eagle with its wings comes stroke our very soul.
And the life we don't live dwindles at every toll,
And there are so many.

O sudden blows! Giddy departure! Mystery!
The many who ignored what should be their query;
Proud, strong, and respected,
Suddenly like a wall comes tumbling to the ground,
Right amid a sentence, a silenced crowd to hound,
By death were selected,

In the immensity who is the eye sublime,
Have turned pale at the sight, in this abyss of time,
Of stars and of azure,
Where the mask is revealed, where the unknown appears,
That whatever they'd done in the face of their peers
Was reaching God, for sure!

A specter at the gate, a finger on his lips,
Smothers his every word, buried in the night, deep.
They dive in the abyss,
Naked, self-diffusing, and not a single glare.
Where is it that they went? Do not ask; don't you dare.
That's it; once you're dismissed.

How did they tread down there? Question deep and hollow!
They go down like the skiff in the ocean below.
Their pale selves fade away,
And you hear nothing more from the thickening gloom
But the sound that emits from the unending doom,
Faint wailing of dismay.

Infinity, dark trail, and cloudy all the way,
Rises and multiplies, man to God to relay,
Its twists and fading ridge,
Then dissipate… the fright takes over suddenly
When faced with the arches, huge piers that solidly
Hold down this immense bridge.

O fate! Obscurity! Brume! We dream; we suffer.
Humans scattered around by what the winds offer,
Ignore what they're doing.
The livings are haggard. The dead are in their pall.
While we're here pondering, teardrops on us come fall
Straight from the dark ceiling.

XIV

We dare the unchanging, then we go in hiding
Either in the slumber or in merrymaking.
Then we utter out loud,
"Down with virtue, duty, and faith! Hollow are men!
In this somber being, like a beast in its den,
Nothing can make one proud.

Listen to him: "Enjoy, that's all. Time does not wait.
Sacrifice is senseless. Martyrdom, insensate.
Living only matters.
Immensity cracks up, and the tomb grimaces.
Life is but a pebble that the wise amasses,
Heaven to throw after."

And the grim convict blows, on the angel, his throes.
Hideous, he enjoys; he drinks, chews, and swallows.
He laughs his well-being,
With all shades of laughter that madness can beget,
He utters what can say, all with hatred beset,
The worm to the Being.

He says no to the One who set the earth's two poles.
Suddenly the angel silently grabs a hold
Of this daring scoffer,
And death comes from behind while he's busy singing.
And all of a sudden, God fills this gape spitting
With eternal stopper.

XV

O winds, what will you do of all this scythed grass?
Whatever will you do with all this straw amassed
And of the cut-down tree?
What will you do of those taken away too soon
And of the one who laughs or who sings a sad tune,
O winds, blowing so free?

What will be of the hearts? What will the souls become?
Alas! We loved one day. We believed; we fathomed.
Once upon we were bright;
In every pantheon, in every ossuary,
We shivered; those with flags or the shrouds they carry
With rags shred well in sight!

And your breath keeps us whole, tears us down, and then gnaws!
We were once full of life; now we're just dreaming raw!
Everything is now gone!
We're no longer aware of the push or the pull.
In vain, we inquire with souls forever full
Of nights of thunder prone!

O winds, what will you do of these swirls of humans,
Old and young, rich and poor, children, women or men,
Suffering and praying,
Loving, doubting, being either ash, either seed,
In their shiver, rolling, all pale, at your own speed,
Heading for the crossing?

XVI

The tree Eternity stands topless and rootless.
With branches all over, near the worm, they caress
Even the golden star.
The space sees unending the growth of branch Number,
And the branch Destiny, with surge ever somber,
Startles humans by far.

We feel it crawl slowly, growing inside our head,
Joining Deutz to Judas, Nimrod to dear Sinead,
Nodding its thousand knots,
And since we are beset with eternal fibers,
Trembling, we see it cross. All the while we slumber,
The giddy threads it caught.

And then we realize, in darker parts of tree,
The Hobbes contemplating with marble eyes to see
The Kant with large faces;
With their axes secured, with foot on the problems,
Immobile, for old death had swallowed all of them,
Changed lumberjack paces.

They're all here and startled and each one on its branch.
One stood up; the other, frightened dove in a trench.
One wanted, and one dared.
All just stopped when they saw the depth of mystery.
Xenon his dream toward Pyrrhus and then Thierry
Turned trying to be paired.

What have you found really, O sublime researchers?
What nest have you noticed, dark abyss on perches
Over knotty branches?
Were they hiding swarms of somber or whitish wings?
Have you disturbed the nest, lost in slumberous swing,
Of eagle in trenches?

For the one who's silent, we stand as ministers;
The dark grid of the fate perturbs our sight luster.
The winds shove everyone;
The shadow every night comes wrap around all heads.
Who then knows the secret, you, winds of mighty stead,
Abyss, with talks undone?

The ever-mute problem swells the tumultuous sea,
And nonstop wavering goes from dusk to dawn see,
And the mole and the lynx.
The riddle sunken eyes keep on us a fixed stare;
In the distant shadow destiny dawning glare
Shows the claws of the sphinx.

The word is God. This Word shines through the widow Soul;
He trembles in the flame. All rivers, He controls.
Man, He runs in your blood;
The stars in unison witness Him in silence.
The volcano spews Him, once given a mere chance,
To stars as sweet accord.

Let's not doubt but believe. Let's fill up all the earth
With blessed faithfulness, humbly spawned from our girth.
Faith dismantles all fears.
Let's not let mere blindness stand as an obstacle;
To the whole creation, offer this spectacle
Of the blind who now peers.

For I'll remind you what your ears refuse to hear:
No is a dark abyss. O people! Death is near,
The flesh goes to the crows.
Life, as we well know it, dwindles day after day.
The lawn is green and soft, but much more nowadays,
More tombs than flowers grow.

As soon as comes the doubt, all appears bleak and sad.
When it wants, gay specter, of cheap sarcasm-clad,
And sadness in the eyes,
To laugh with the immense, poor soul bearing boredom,
The human shivering sees around God's kingdom
And the mountain's true size.

Under the cedar stare, the moved oak takes a bow;
The dreamy rock mimics all that the priest avows.
His mercy to afford,
The spider, immobile, dangling between its webs,
Ponders; and the lion, dosing under star pleb,
Roars softly, "Pity, Lord!"

Regrets

Once upon in lifetime, as though to prove a point
That the power of love still befalls the conjoint,
Two souls gladly surfing over this world's meadows,
Hand in hand, relieving one another's sorrow,

Glowing in blissful might, gleaming of the same light,
Emanating a sun, forever warm and bright,
Living one and the same, basking in sweet glory,
Dazzled, like exiting some enchanted story,

Where this pair of lovebirds, with borrowed rays of sun,
Would, in their ecstasy, the rest of us, just shun.
If ever they would be from themselves drawn apart,
They'd resourcefully steer toward their counterpart
And, in a sweet sudden, daring the daunting crowd,
Dash toward the other then soar above the clouds…

Oh yes, I had once known the true love of my life.
You dream of her embrace so often and so true.
And at the crack of dawn, despite your fiercest strife,
She flies, leaving you her sweet dew.

You yearn for her return down some flowery trail.
You send silent clamors on your knees night and day.
But when you hear the knock, sadly it never fails
To be just mirages that stray'.

And if in my weakness I were to let them in,
That would be of my time such a waste and a lost.
I'd pay for my beloved with regrets deep within,
But remorse has a higher cost.

Don't call her name to me; don't rekindle the flame.
Don't speak of this old time when I was once complete,
For the sound of my voice would never be the same
When I remember my defeat.

Everyone deep inside harbors within their soul
A lost love and so learned to stifle the deep sighs.
We all carry a cross, paying subtly a toll,
Once our chance has passed us by.

This love boat, in lifetime, only once docks your shore;
Blessed is the pilgrim it finds keen and ready!
Whenever it departs, much loaded than before,
You suffer your loss already.

We sober silently; we make all kind of deals.
We beg for an encore, a replay of the scene.
But forward we all go; nothing's at a standstill.
Only the Lord can intervene.

She flew, my Tweedy Bird, without leaving a trace,
But she sings in my heart at every crack of dawn.
And still at my window I hope to see her face,
Sweetly skipping upon my lawn…

Oh yes, I had once known the true love of my life.
I dream of her embrace so often and so true.
At each crack of my dawn, despite my fiercest strife,
I wake up missing her anew.

Summer Night

And the night all muffled, hovering, conniving,
Glittered its canopy of diamonds, flickering,
With colluding shadows smothering the whispers,
And the soft-scented breeze stroking your blushing cheek
All seem to land a hand to bring us to this peak
And make of us a pair.

I remained standing there, all ablaze in my love,
And you were just gazing, glowing in the midst of
Some borrowed tender ease revamping your sweet face.
All lost in this charming attire that the night,
Silently over you, poured with its eerie light;
Genuine heavenly grace.

Deep inside I gave thanks to my most gracious Lord
For this most blessed night enrobing this accord.
Nothing could say better the core of His nature.
A blessed night of nights and your face, my delight,
And the golden silence, all reflecting His might
Way beyond known measures.

God is the only source of every known beauty.
God is the only font of every good bounty.
Blessed be His sweet name, He who so lovingly,
Knowing all well the depths of my feelings for you,
Set up this magic night tailor-made for us two;
All done ingeniously.

Nothing on His green earth springs up without His touch.
Nothing would stay alive if His Spirit were hushed.
He created sweet love and sprouts it as solace
Deeply within the hearts of those He sees merits.
So with His sole blessing, they can treasure its treats
Given to every race.

Let yourself be enthralled. Don't you forsake the bliss.
Don't let life pass you by on such a night as this.
Come alive, my sweet dove. Come claim the blessed crown
That since heaven above has it sealed with your name.
It glitters specially to fit your lovely frame,
Devoid of any frown.

Wisdom states that solely what can the spirit, tame
Remains heavenly love, not riches and not fame.
Amass all that you can of bullions of pure gold,
Be famous and renowned the whole world and beyond,
Never will you attain the joys of this sweet bond,
So of it grab a hold.

Love's realm is spiritual, therefore everlasting.
It obeys to no law. It's sweeter when its stings,
Knows no race, no boundary, gains strength over the years,
Takes roots no one knows when, and blooms with sweet nothings;
A glance, a tender touch, a poem among all things,
All set by God, my dear.

Under God's loving eye, solely on His goodness,
When He made old Adam, He flanked him a mistress.
Tis law of His nature; hand in hand all things go.
The poem has melody; the heavens have the earth.
The blue sky has the sea to reflect gloom or mirth;
Love makes the spirit glow.

Wisdom V.H.

I

So then nothing will spring, nothing grand, nothing pure,
Nothing worthy, O Lord, of your eye of azure!
Nothing that ennobles, the base time we live in,
Will emerge from the heart of any human being!
Human! Spirit buried under the body's needs!
Just enjoy! Then descend, stifled down by his greed,

Be part of all that crawls, everything that's petty,
To the cheap benefits, the trivial, the flighty,
To know nothing but fill, with no moral concern,
A charter with just words or bank with cash return.

Never look up to watch the starry dome at night,
To enjoy devotion and the virtues' true might;
This is your life, alas! Night and day, all you save,
As a goal and for hope, to worship and to rave,
Is an unclean treasure, amassed from sordid gains,
That leaves your soul baffled, dejected, crestfallen!

And you can never grasp that your own destiny
Is to think! To become a magus if any,
A king, an alchemist feeding the very flame
Under this fragile still that has soul as its name,
And after you distill, with fire under pod,
Nature and the whole world, you simply pull out God!

What! The beast has its sphere; the element, its rule!
The sea, its cormorant; the snow, the eagle rules.
Everything has its goal, its region, its function.
The spume up from the waves is pure ebullition.
The tide knows its duty; the wind knows where to blow,
Like a temple that bathes from a pale light aglow.
The obedient brilliance of stars gives sky clearness.
The lily comes and blooms from the Lord's blessedness.

Each and every morning, like a rhythmic lyre,
The bird sings His sweet name that the dawn transpires.
What! Man is full of love; the world is so sincere!
Everything around us under God's law is dear

And knows not to obey, resting on divine pride
Bird to its mere instinct; the tree, the roots it hides!
What! The immense ocean rises up to its shores.
What! The bird in the north, the south, the magnet stores,

The flying grain landing in a spot of its choice,
The huge clouds hovering on icy lands with poise,
Traveling the big sky, riding to God's meter,
Melt under April's zest, down to the equator,

The iceberg gliding down from white-mountain summits,
The sap evenly spread in branches' tiny bits,
All created objects for a serious purpose,
The rays piecing the air, the many stars in pause,

The rivers running down through the rocks and the grass,
Go steady on their paths set up from ages past!
Man alone went astray! What! The whole universe,
All the mounts, the livings, the forests so dispersed,

The day bleaching the sky, the sea reaching the shores,
Continue, like the day, in a blessed encore.
The Lord over Adam impressed His gracious might,
Bathing in innocence, in candor and delight!

Only man has fallen! Carved straight from divine love,
For emerging the best, he ended the worst off.
He, designed to flourish as sublime tree of choice,
Is but a rotten trunk, belching a hollow noise,

Uprooted by the years and worn out by vices,
And whose branches produce fruits heaven despises,
Against whom one can lean at his risks and perils
And where society comes strong passions instill!

Deep abyss! He ignores and denies, O dear God!
Whereas all around him, creation weighs her rod!
What a shame! Under yokes of enslaving senses,
Man vegetates meanwhile creation still prances.

II

Just as I was bugging, you heard me ventilate,
And you, shining amid all you articulate,
You turned toward me then with face with peace glowing
And a most saddened smile, ineffable, calming.

Human nature rises then tumbles all anew
And, with a sullied face, still looks for dawn brand-new.
Everyone on this earth has two faces, the good
And the bad. Blaming all means we've misunderstood.

The souls of the humans are of gold and of lead.
The wise mind rests heavy, ponders the world with stead,
And does not fulminate for no reason at all.
In this time where laughter and sorrow can befall,

Alas! One is always unjust. All is a crime.
This era sad and vile has a side so sublime.
And you said it yourself, O you troubled poet!
In your famous dwelling, and of respect beset,
This is how you put it serene and yet simple.
Your face with the aspect of damask, all dimpled,
Was glowing, and for me at this precious moment,
Your glance to the ceiling brought down the firmament.

The mark of reflection, august and pacific,
Justice, heartfelt pity, goodness so angelic,
Offense forgetfulness, that most precious virtue
That ennobles a man unaware of his due,

Tinted your every word, enticing, enthralling,
With a peaceful grandeur of all natural things,
And at times would appear, to mingle with your voice,
These soft and muttered airs that all forests, rejoice.

III

Why this constant recall over my troubled mind,
O days of my childhood, joy that I left behind?
Who bring you steadily back to our writhen hearts,
O luminous flower, souvenirs to impart?

Oh! How happy I was! Oh! How I was candid!
In school, on bench of oak, used, lustrous, and splendid,
A table, a small desk, a heavy black inkstand,
A lamp, lonely sibling of the night star at hand

Would welcome me softly and rather seriously.
My teacher was a priest; I said repeatedly
With calm and soothing voice and warm, embracing stare,
Naive as an expert, cunning as boy can dare,

Who'd welcome me saying, for any praise excites,
"Although he's only nine, Tacitus he recites."
Then next to dear Eugene, whose spirit God assumed,
I would work peacefully with thoughts with hint of gloom

While already writing, freely but with no shape,
Pouring faults all over on anything I'd tape,
Inventing to authors some unexpected wits,
My back bent and the face resting against my fist.

I once thought, for always the child mind's vigilant,
I could hear whispering, at any clear instant,
The Latin and Greek words that were so familiar
With ink spots all over, happy as young scholars,

Whispering as do birds on branch, stationary,
Between the dark pages of some dictionary.
Sounding so much softer than a swarm flying by,
With murmurs more muttered than the average night's sigh,

That would cause to shiver, at times, even while closed,
Vaguely, the old pages of books of rhymes or prose!
Once homework's done, happy, as could be three young deers,
We would run up and down the gardens without fear,

Shouting all three of us, each against the other.
I, with uneven steps, would follow my brothers,
And the night's serene stars would light up the dark sky.
And the flies would all buzz softly when they'd come by,

And the peaceful swallow, singing in the shadow,
Teaching the world around how to keep a solo,
While we, talkative kids, gesturing all over,
Searching the world around set out to discover,

From where was just glowing some lively inner zest,
I'd carry, under arm, tied up by three string nets,
Horace and the festins, Virgil and the forests,
Olympus, Theseus, Hercules, and Ceres
And Juno, the cruel one, the Lernaean hydra beast,
The humongous lion of the town of Nemea.

But when I would return back home to my mother,
All thanks to this sheer luck, tricking one another,
I was always so sad and at times so damn mad.
I couldn't find anymore, once placed on some small pad,

The cute little garden set up with so much care.
Some big dog came around. Oh! This I could not bear.
Or someone in my room came open the cages
And all my birds had flown, heading for boscages

To happily go flit from flower to flower,
Enjoying their freedom, trying their wing power.
O Lord! Then I would run, red, all lost and rapid,
Damning the blasted dog, the gardener too stupid,

As well as that damn cage and its repulsive strands,
Furious! One mother's look would have my mouth retrained.

IV

Nowadays, it is not because of empty cage,
Or because of my birds flown to some tree boscage
Or some big dog barking, my flowers destroying
That I flare up this way. No, the smallest of things

A child comes unsettle, but just like when in church,
Dealing with heavy prongs, one maintains a deep hush
After crushing sadness, just like from a hot day,
Just like the heart settles, one comes fall on his hay.

To all woe somber count, wisdom is the great sum.
Through their tribulations, God seems to say to some,
"Allow your soul the prongs under which it succumbs.
Like the grain through the sieve, it'd grow better when numb."

I have lived, I suffered, in peace now I linger.
Or if at times again, some uncontrolled anger
Comes tilt the quiescence with skills of a winner
Of this peaceful feeling, this quiet demeanor;

If with a clouded eye, I condemn and I blame,
With a few calming words, you sweet and noble dame,
You'd bring down my shouting fueled by my annoyance
To the calm I treasure, my pledge of allegiance.

I feel that your soft rays, my fury can just tame,
And you do for the man, on verge of losing fame,
What did my mother then to this unsettled kid,
With one look from her eyes, made him calm and limpid!

V

Now listen to me well! In my noisy dwelling,
At times, in turn, others, together, expelling,
Three voices, right aloud murmur. And then one said,
"Get angry at yourself, poet. Yes hell has okayed

All that this century sketches, creates, attempts.
Stay indignant! This time dwells in an impure tent,
Where one draws to himself, at the fall of the dusk,
Sensuousness of the flesh and vice infamous tusk.

The truth that in the past made a beacon of Rome
Hovers still in heaven; love shines under His dome.
Every ray of brightness finds self blindfolded eyes.
Oh! Do not push away the muse coming with prize

Who often visited, like an austere old friend,
Amos and Jeremy, somber giants of then!
Human beings are barren, wicked, liars, jealous.
Crime's in many of us; vanity's hideous.

For from the sap we drink branches of the same vine,
Some favor Cain, but still in all of us Eve shines.
"My Lord! Your cross tumbles, and then respect departs.
Prayer is losing ground. Chill invaded the hearts!

They come calling your name out loud in your temple.
The book portrayed the law, the priest, the example.
Book and priest are gone now. Even faith nowadays,
This torch lit as beacon in every hearth that prays,

Which, marking for your Christ, the ones He selected,
Long ago purified the twelve He elected,
Is but a lifeless coal used by daring young brats
To sully your great wall, giggling at the mere act."

The other voice, "Forgive! Love! God that we revere!
God, to the contrite soul, will never be severe.
"Respect the ant much less than you do the lion.
Airhead! Nothing is small with the mark of Zion.

The universal being rises from the atom.
God is within us all. This many don't fathom.
Cultivate deep in you love, pity. Be serene,
And if fate forces you to closely examine

The frivolous human, blinded and so reckless,
Calms the eye of the judge with the sadness express'
By his brother. That here, the air, flower, and grass,
The happy bunch playing under your window glass,

The poor man, outside begging on the sidewalk,
"The birds perched on the branch, cooing in a sweet talk,
The old books on the wharf whose pages the wind blows,
Revealing the great thoughts of ancient wise men's prose,

Fly by and come landing on your receptive mind,
The impressive concerns that these women remind
When you see them sobbing, like the algae, drowning,
Human the spectator, the world, this great drawing,

"Allow these august scenes, for the common, blasé,
Day after day, come move your life in ecstasy
Toward the All-seeing, scoping His creation,
Invisible and keen, in perpetual motion!

"Principle, goal, medium! Clarity, warmth, sweet balm,
Secret for everything, who every soul, embalms!
Don't ignite any hell with brand of any fire.
Don't add to no one's load. Bring all to admire

"God, the spirit, the soul, the irrevocable tomb
And ease for everyone, where they often succumb,
The Word whose yoke is light but who solemnly writes,
"Never," on all the tombs. "Always," as altar rites."

The third voice said, "To love, to hate? What's the big deal!
Sing or repudiate, enter or leave. For real!
Good, evil, death, vices, the gods, all the above,
Does it really bother the great Giver of Love?

"The bright vegetation, always blind and somber,
Has ever lost foliage or its trees in number,
In lichens and in grass, in seaweeds and in plants,
The fields and the meadows, the sea and rocks He grants?

"Is the sea lesser blue? Do forests have less lawn?
Does the breeze, any less, in the shadow, at dawn,
Over the horizons or when waves get meaner,
Carry these happy clouds in all the four corners?

"The sun brightly shining through the lovely seasons
For kings in their castles, for convicts in prison,
Does it lose its splendor that it was once beset,
Any corner on which its warm ray does not set?

No! Pan has no such need to be prayed or be loved.
O Wisdom, pure spirit! Supreme being from above!
Zeus! Irminsul! Vishnu! Jupiter! Jehovah!
Searched for by Socrates but that Jesus reveals!

"One God! True God! Indeed! One mystery, one soul!
You who brought on the earth what death in her grasp holds
Created the heavens for your eternity!
You who put in the sky all these solemn gaieties,

Tent under which your breath moves every somber veil,
Into millions of birds and millions stars unveil!
What can do, O Mighty, those foolish human beings,
All lost in their darkness, on each other bumping,
Phantoms that forever Your eyes do not recall,
Before Your face glowing, ghosts that stumble and fall?"

VI

In my somber alcove, under my green curtain,
Shines like a dear old friend a book I entertain,
Where my hidden Bible winks at my old Virgil,
I hear these three voices. If my brain, standing still,

Gets startled, I persist. And ever fearlessly,
I let them do in me what they see fit freely.
For human beings baffled by these transformations
Make up their own wisdom based on intuitions.

They all claim loud and clear that they have found the truth,
Each one at his window demanding to see proof.
But no one is tempted by this rock so sublime
To go around and see and on its summit, climb.

And this three-facet prong of things upon the earth,
These three warnings uttered rendering them so deaf,
For my heart where resides my God, where hate dissolves,
Springs a global goodness that with sweetness evolves.

It gilds just like the dawn and renders much tender
The verse that half written I carry and ponder
To go into the fields amid sweet smell of grass,
Finish it in the shade, watching the hours pass.

*My most sincere gratitude to the Dover
Publications Inc. for having allowed me to dive
into their so rich collection of illustrations!*